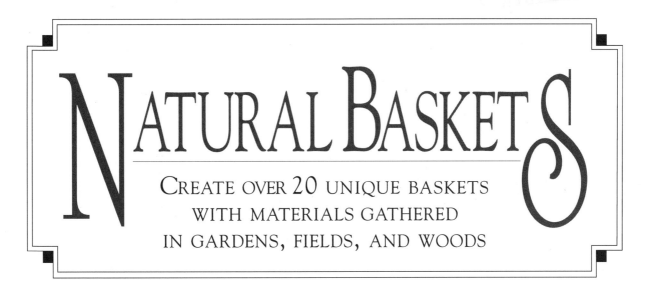

NATURAL BASKETS

CREATE OVER 20 UNIQUE BASKETS
WITH MATERIALS GATHERED
IN GARDENS, FIELDS, AND WOODS

Edited by Maryanne Gillooly

Illustrated by Brigita Fuhrmann

A Storey Publishing Book

STOREY

Storey Communications, Inc.
Schoolhouse Road
Pownal, Vermont 05261

*The mission of Storey Communications is to serve our customers
by publishing practical information that encourages personal independence
in harmony with the environment.*

Cover and text design by Carol Jessop
Cover photograph by A. Blake Gardner
Production by Carol Jessop
Edited by Gwen W. Steege
Color section photographs by A. Blake Gardner, unless otherwise noted
Indexed by Kathleen D. Bagioni

The information in this book is true and complete to the best of our knowledge. All recommendations are made without guarantee on the part of the authors or Storey Communications, Inc. The authors and publisher disclaim any liability with the use of this information. For additional information please contact Storey Communications, Inc., Schoolhouse Road, Pownal, Vermont 05261.

Storey Publishing books are available for special premium and promotional uses and for customized editions. For further information, please call the Customized Publishing Department at 1-800-793-9396.

Printed in the United States by Vicks Lithograph & Printing
10 9 8 7 6 5

Library of Congress Cataloging-in-Publication Data

Natural baskets / edited by Maryanne Gillooly : illustrated by Brigita Fuhrmann.
       p.   cm.
    "A Storey Publishing book."
    Includes bibliographical references and index.
    ISBN 0-88266-793-9 (pbk.)
    1. Basket making.   I. Gillooly, Maryanne, 1951-
TT879.B3N38   1992
746.41'2—dc20   91-51126
                                     CIP

CONTENTS

ABOUT THE AUTHORS

Nancy Basket, a Native American of Cherokee descent, creates contemporary baskets based on traditional designs and techniques. Nancy recently received a grant from the South Carolina Arts Commission to write a book on "Contemporary Cherokee Coiled Basketry Patterns." Along with her teaching and her basketry business, Kudzu Kabin Designs, she has occasionally been commissioned to make authentic props for film and television productions, including a recent film version of *The Last of the Mohicans*. Nancy lives in Jonesville, South Carolina.

Maryanne Gillooly is a basket maker and a floral designer. She has exhibited in galleries and museums in the South and Northeast and taught in regional convention workshops, in public schools, and in several rehabilitation centers. Maryanne lives in New Marlboro, Massachusetts.

Gerrie Kennedy is the Resident Basket Maker at the Hancock (MA) Shaker Village. She has taught courses in basket making at various schools and museums along the East Coast and is a self-employed basket weaver. A contributor to *Simple Gifts* (Storey Communications, 1990), she is also author of *Shaker Baskets*, a resource guide that defines and identifies authentic Shaker baskets (Berkshire House Press, 1992). Gerrie lives in Worthington, Massachusetts.

Diana Macomber has given basketry workshops through the Smithsonian Institution, the National Park Service, and many basketry guilds. Her main basketry interest is weaving Canada geese decoys. British by birth, Diana now resides in Alexandria, Virginia.

Doris Messick is a frequent workshop leader at both national and regional basketry conventions, and she has also taught seminars on basket photography. For thirteen years, she taught at a vocational rehabilitation center for emotionally and intellectually handicapped adults. She is particularly interested in researching the plants used for basketry. She lives in Cambridge, Maryland.

Cass Schorsch is a full-time basket maker, specializing in tree barks and black ash traditional and contemporary baskets. She is a regular workshop leader at several regional basket conferences, and has taught courses at The Basketry School (Seattle, WA), the Basket Gathering (Mowana, OH), and the Rome Symposium (Rome, NY). Cass lives in Ludington, Michigan.

Sandy Whalen has taught adult education courses in Michigan public schools, as well as basketry workshops at various basketry conventions, crafts shops, and basketry guilds throughout the country. She is especially devoted to the growing of basket willow. Sandy lives in Milford, Michigan.

INTRODUCTION
MARYANNE GILLOOLY

For centuries, we human beings have created baskets to serve many functions — for storage, for gathering the harvest, for trapping fish and game, and for collecting and carrying our belongings. Baskets are so integral to our needs that they serve as vessels in the most basic rites and rituals of our lives — carrying us at birth, serving us in life, and transporting us to our place of rest at death. Perhaps it is because of this long history that we instinctively appreciate baskets not only for their function but also for their beauty. There is even something special about the *feel* of baskets! They seem to offer us comfort and balance. How can we resist swinging one from an arm as we go to gather vegetables or flowers from the garden?

I am continually amazed by the variety of baskets I see in museums, galleries, and antique shops. Some are simple, woven quickly to serve an immediate purpose; others are carefully planned and executed to provide many years of service and durability. The materials of which they are made range from rough-textured bark to smooth, finely cut splints. Depending upon the purpose of the basket, the weavers are tiny and intricately woven or wide and openly spaced. Whether coiled, plaited, twined, or woven, each basket tells a story of the maker and the materials. More than mere containers, baskets, like their creators, are what is *inside* as well as what is *outside*. Even empty, they reveal their wonders both inside and out.

Traditionally, basket makers have taken plants and trees indigenous to an area to create their baskets. Nature *still* provides us with an endless supply of materials virtually right outside our doors. By exploring the fields, marshes, stream beds, and wooded areas, we can seek out these free and plentiful weaving materials. This search can reawaken our senses, and we can see and learn from nature. When we do this, we soon become aware that every bit of nature is unique, and that every geographical region offers vast possibilities, each with its own characteristics of color, texture, and form. It is this variety that makes working with natural materials so inspiring and rewarding.

This book encourages us to experience the joy of harvesting our own materials. Going directly to nature for materials becomes an enticing endeavor. Each of the contributors to this book describes how to identify, cut, prepare, and work with the natural materials she uses. Potential basketry materials include birch bark, pine needles, willow, and vines — even unexpected materials, like Diana Macomber's equisetum shoots and Gerrie Kennedy's horsehair.

For each basket maker, the gathering of materials is an important part of the basket making process itself, for without that step, a certain spirit would be lost. By sharing the gifts that natural basket making has to offer, these basket makers hope to not only pass on the ways in which they express their own creativity, but also encourage us to look at nature, become inspired by it, gather a little of it in our arms, and create our own unique baskets.

If the materials in a specific project are not available in every area, the authors often suggest alternatives and encouragement to experiment with whatever we can find where we live. In addition, not only can we search out wonderful weaving materials, but we can sometimes take some home and grow the plants in our own gardens — we would all love a willow patch like Sandy Whalen's! With the helpful advice of Sandy and other authors, we can plant, care for, and maintain a basket garden full of our own basket weaving materials.

Although these baskets can also be constructed of manufactured or processed materials, nature provides us with wonderful forms and color patterns that are hard to compete with. For instance, the plaited birch-bark baskets of Cass Schorsch just would not be the same if made of reed or splints, for they would lack the unique and varied patterns found in the bark she weaves with; Doris Messick's nontraditional use of twisted vines, philodendron, and yucca is what gives her rib-constructed baskets their distinctive character; Nancy Basket's choice of a different plant materials for each of her six coiled baskets gives every one a different look and feel.

In addition to the oportunity to choose from a wealth of materials to create a basket, we can also begin, weave, and complete a basket in many different ways. Each author gives clear directions that share her own special techniques, helpful diagrams, and alternatives to guide you in your own efforts. Although basketry is an acquired skill, however, its methods are simple and straightforward. There really are no rules or limitations—no right or wrong. We have so many rules and restrictions in our every day lives, we do not need to inflict them on our creative lives as well! So, do not hesitate to alter these designs, materials, and methods. It is in developing your own personal style and rhythm that you create work that has spirit and character, and the innovative features of your project can transform an ordinary basket into a work of art.

I encourage you to enjoy the process as well as the finished product. Basket weaving is an intimate art of rhythm, form, and time. What you feel and *how* you create matters as much as *what* you create. Whether you try your hand at a miniature horsehair basket, an old-fashioned bee skep, or a traditional English willow basket, the completed piece becomes a record of you, the weaver, as well as of the time spent.

It is evident through their expression of connection not only with their work but with nature itself that the basket artists who contributed to this book love weaving baskets by hand — enjoying both the time spent and the pleasure of interacting with the materials. This love of nature brings with it the desire to care for the natural world and preserve it, so that generations of basket makers can find inspiration and resources in its wonderful gifts.

WEAVING BASKETS WITH EQUISETUM

DIANA MACOMBER

I was first attracted to *Equisetum* when I saw it growing alongside a road in upstate New York. We stopped the car and I quickly picked a bundle, as we had a twelve-hour journey ahead of us and I looked forward to experimenting with what appeared to be a weavable plant. It did not need to be immersed in water (an asset when travelling by car), and I was able to make several little baskets on the long drive home.

Equisetum is the botanical name for a deep green, stiff-jointed rush variously known as horsetail, Tinker Toy, pewterwort, and scouring rush. The last two common names originate because in American Colonial times, bundles of horsetail were used for polishing pewter or scouring pots. Children enjoy pulling apart its bamboolike segments. Herbalists list many beneficial uses for this plant, and gardeners find that horsetail "tea" is an effective natural fungicide. Used as a dye plant, it gives a good shade of yellow. Best of all, it is reported that if you burn horsetail grown around old silver mines, you will find silver dust in the ashes.

In height 18 to 24 inches, the variety that I use has no side branches. It grows in both thick and sparse patches, in wasteland or on sandy banks in full sun, as well as in dense shade under pine trees. Although some of the plants in a stand die back, I have been able to pick strong green rushes at all times of year. If transplanted to your garden and kept moist, equisetum will flourish and spread by underground runners.

In all likelihood, farmers will gladly give you permission to pick all the horsetail you want from their land, as it is bad for grazing animals. To collect, give each rush a gentle tug to bring it up with a very short root, or cut it off at the base. Horsetail remains flexible for several days if wrapped in burlap or paper sacks

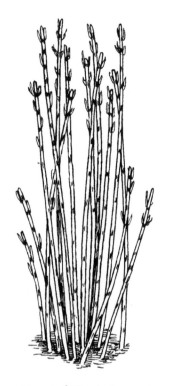

Horsetail (*Equisetum* sp.)

and kept in a cool place. Do not store it in plastic, as this encourages mold. If you wish to keep a supply in ready-to-use condition for long periods, however, you can store it in the freezer in plastic leaf bags. You may also spread the horsetail out until it is dry, and then store it in paper bags in a cool, dry place. Dry horsetail will need to be soaked for about eight hours before use.

The rushes are a rich color when first gathered, but like all natural plant greens, over several weeks horsetail baskets turn shades of pale green and straw. Fading is hastened by exposure to sunlight.

Other pliable weavers are honeysuckle (*Lonicera* spp.) and wisteria (*Wisteria* spp.). I particularly like the latter's long runners that lie on the surface of the ground. Both are best gathered from October through March. Use them right after gathering, or store them dry and soak them for a few hours before use. Honeysuckle is strengthened and becomes more pliable if boiled for three hours before it is stored.

Some of the baskets in this chapter include alternate materials that can be purchased from basketry supply houses (see page 151 for addresses). These include imported, processed rattan reed, which comes in 1-pound bundles in numbered sizes, and vine rattan, which is not ordered by size, but has variations within each bundle. Vine rattan has a very natural look, which blends well with gathered materials. Both reed and vine rattan should be soaked in water for a few minutes before weaving. As you weave, dip the basket in water occasionally or spray it with water.

The equipment needed for weaving with horsetail is extremely basic — a bowl of water and sharp scissors or small garden snippers.

Following are instructions for three twined baskets. Begin with the first little basket, which is the simplest, so that you get used to handling the material. My philosophy for working with natural materials is that you should not try to be too precise or to make exact copies of other baskets. Enjoy yourself. Although you do need to master the weaving techniques, allow the vines some will of their own. Remember when reading my instructions that I may have used a bundle of reeds that are thinner or thicker than yours, so the measurements will not be exact. Also, I may have used wisteria spokes, whereas you may want to use honeysuckle. Say, "This is *my* version of *that* basket." You will soon be designing your own.

TWINING WITH HORSETAIL

Horsetail rush is flexible, yet stiff. This stiffness makes it unsuitable for simple randing (a single weaver going over and under), but it has a very attractive nubby texture when **twined.** In twining, you work simultaneously with two weavers that emerge from adjoining spaces between spokes. The weaver on the left crosses over both the spoke on its right and the weaver on its right, passes behind the next spoke and out to the front. This is repeated with the second weaver.

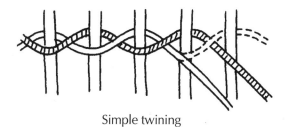

Simple twining

When you get close to the end of a rush weaver (4 or 5 inches from the tip), start a new one right alongside. If you end with a tip, start with a tip; if you end with a butt, start with a butt. Leave the old end sticking out, to be trimmed off later.

MATERIALS

SPOKES

Wisteria runners, vine rattan, or #4 reed: six 20" lengths

WEAVERS

Thin wisteria, vine rattan, or #3 reed: 90"

Horsetail rush: 30 stems

SMALL HORSETAIL BASKET
5" diameter x 3" high

This small basket (shown on color page 87) is a good project for beginners.

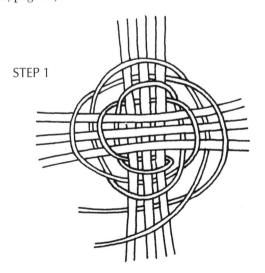

BASKET BODY

1. Cross three 20-inch spokes over the other three spokes at their centers. Take a long weaver (wisteria, vine rattan, or #3 reed), fold it in the center and loop it around the bottom set of three spokes. Treating each group of three as one unit, twine around the spokes for three complete rounds. (See Twining with Horsetail, page 3.)

STEP 1

2. Separate the spokes, and twine between single spokes for two rounds.

3. Cut off ends of both weavers and tuck to inside.

4. Take two of the horsetail rushes, and tuck their thick ends under the spokes about 2 inches before the end of the wisteria weavers. Stagger the ends so that they begin under adjoining spokes. Start twining with the horsetail. (The rest of the basket will be woven with horsetail.)

5. When the diameter of the base measures 5 inches, bend the spokes so they go straight up, and weave four or five more rounds to form the sides. Every so often, spread your fingers between the spokes and push down on the rows of weaving to keep them tightly packed.

STEP 2

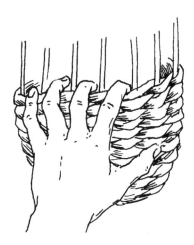

STEP 5

6. Trim off the loose ends inside and outside of the basket.

7. Hold the spokes inward, so that the top of the basket curves in as you weave.

8. Weave about five more rounds until the top opening measures 3 inches across. Tuck the ends of the two horsetail weavers to the inside.

STEP 7

MAKING THE BORDER

9. Cut all the spokes to measure 2½ inches from the top of the weaving. Turn the basket upside down, and soak it in 3 inches of water for five minutes, until the spoke ends are pliable.

10. Beginning with any one spoke, bend it in *front* of the spoke immediately on its right, and then lay it *behind* the spoke to the right of that one. Continue in this manner, moving around the rim in a counterclockwise direction. Although the spokes in the drawing are shown loose in order to illustrate construction, they should be pulled tight in actual weaving.

STEP 10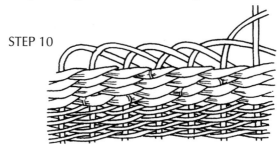

11. When you get to the last spoke, keep to this pattern, passing in front of the first spoke you bent over and tucking it behind the next one.

12. Trim off any weaver ends or spoke ends that look too long. (They must, however, at least overlap the adjoining spoke or they will pop out on the wrong side.)

13. If the bottom of your basket needs leveling, soak it for five minutes, and then turn it upside down and either push in on the base with your thumbs or leave a flat weight on it until it is dry.

BROKEN SPOKES

If a spoke should break while you are weaving, simply sharpen the end of a new piece of spoke and slide it into the weaving alongside the broken one for about 2 inches. Cut the old broken spoke off at the end of the weaving, and carry on.

broken spoke

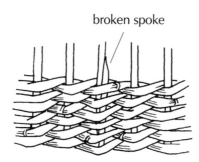

OPENWORK BASKET

13" diameter x 8" high

Generous and elegant, this openwork basket (shown on color page 87) offers opportunities to create your own unique design.

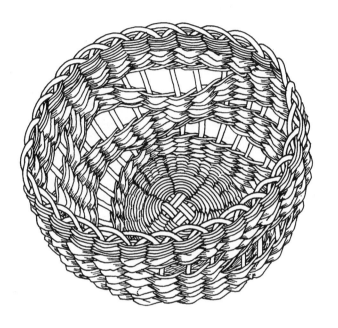

SPOKES

Oval oval ¼" reed: sixteen 36" lengths

WEAVERS

#2 round reed: ¼ pound

#0 round reed: 2 ounces (about 20 yards)

Horsetail rush: about seventy 20" stems

Straight florist's wire: 24"

CREATING THE BASE

1. To create Base 1, take eight of the 36-inch lengths of the oval oval reed, and cross them in pairs at the centers, as in the illustration. Take a long piece of #2 reed, fold it over at its center and twine around the pairs of spokes for twelve rounds. Pack in the twining firmly as you weave. Cut off weavers, and set Base 1 aside.

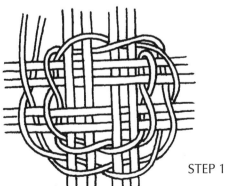

STEP 1

2. To create Base 2, repeat Step 1 with the remaining spokes, *except do not* cut off the weavers.

3. Place Base 1 flat inside Base 2, so that the center holes are matched up and the spokes fan out, with four from Base 1 alternating with four from Base 2 all around. Base 2 will be the outside of the basket. With Base 2 held toward you, continue twining with the weavers round all pairs of spokes. Do this for three rounds, keeping the base flat.

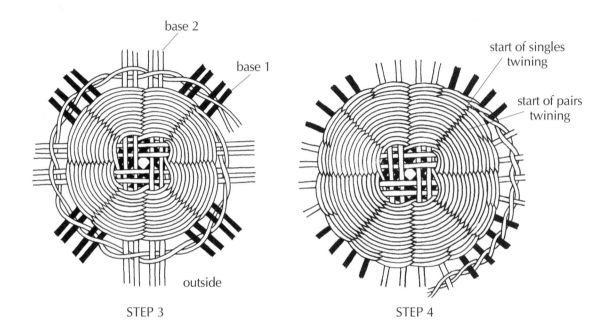

STEP 3

STEP 4

4. Separate the spokes, and continue twining between each of them for two more rounds. Cut off weavers and leave ends inside basket. Set this framework aside.

PREPARING THE HORSETAIL WEAVERS

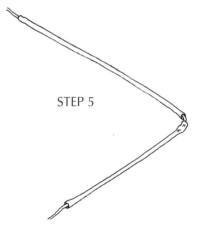

STEP 5

5. Because the horsetail rushes that are the weavers have to span open spaces between the spokes, they require some special preparation to convert them into long, unbroken lengths. Cut the tips off each end of all the rushes. Insert the florist's wire into the narrow end of a rush, push it down to the wide end, and withdraw it. Take a long strand of #0 reed, point the end, and thread it through the rushes, one by one, to create a long string of rushes, end to end. Knot the reed at both ends to prevent the rushes from slipping off. Make several long horsetail weavers in this manner.

WEAVING THE BASKET SIDES

6. Rest the basket on its side in your lap with the base toward you. Hold the spokes curved in the shape you wish the basket to take. Starting where you left off with the reed weavers, use two long strands of horsetail to twine two complete rounds.

7. Following the pattern shown, continue twining with rush, but now carry the twining up and leave a space between the old and new rows of weaving for three or four spokes. Next, bring the twining down and weave against the row below for four or more spokes. Continue in this way, creating three spaces the first time around. Alongside this row, twine another one touching the previous row all the way around.

8. Weave three more double rounds of twining, creating random spaces as you twine up the sides of the basket. Always make at least two rows of horsetail bordering each space.

9. When the diameter of the basket measures about 13 inches, start curving the sides inward.

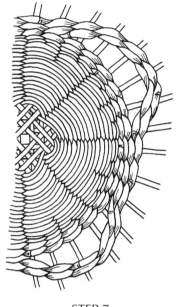

STEP 7

10. When the height of the basket reaches 7 inches, stop twining with horsetail rush and change to #2 reed. Weave two rows of twining against the last row of rush.

11. Staying with the reed, make three or more spaces and finish weaving by making five solid rows of twined reed. Make sure that you continue to curve the spokes inward, and so shape the basket in this last stage. Snip off the ends of the weavers, laying them to the inside of the basket.

DELINEATING THE SPACES

12. Take a 36-inch piece of #0 reed, and fold it at the middle around a spoke at one corner of one of the spaces. Twine completely around the open space, and cut off the reed at the corner where you began. Repeat for all spaces. This delineates each space.

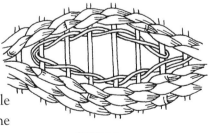

STEP 12

MAKING THE BORDER

13. To make the border, trim the protruding spokes to 4 inches long; cut the ends to a point. Turn the basket upside down, and soak the spokes in water for a few minutes.

14. Grasp any spoke, bring it in front of the one on its right, and tuck it down behind the following right hand spoke, inside the last five rows of twining. Repeat all the way around.

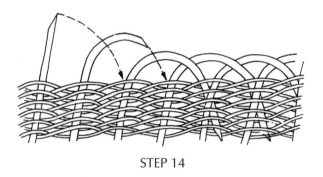

STEP 14

15. Trim off the spoke ends where they protrude beyond the weaving.

LEVELING THE BASKET

If your basket does not sit flat, wet the base, set the basket right side up on newspaper on a firm surface. Place a round weight (such as a can of beans with another weight on top of it) in the center, and let it sit until it is dry.

NUT BASKET

8" diameter x 5½" high

This makes an attractive gift basket filled with unshelled hazelnuts or other nuts. You may wish to dye the reed and vine rattan to add color contrast.

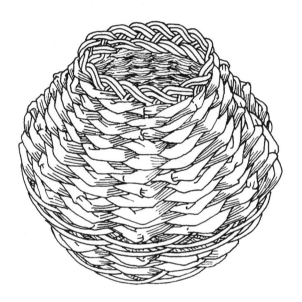

MATERIALS

SPOKES

#5 round reed: eight 36" lengths

Vine rattan: sixteen thin 8" pieces (bye stakes)

WEAVERS

Vine rattan: thirty-two 60" pieces

Horsetail rush: thirty 30" or longer pieces

CREATING THE BASE

1. Cross four spokes over four at their centers. To help you count rounds, mark the first spoke with a twist tie or colored thread. Double over your thinnest piece of vine rattan, and make two

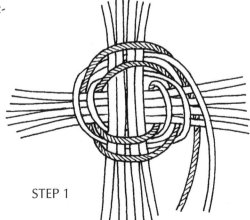

STEP 1

rounds of twining, including four spokes in each group.

2. Take a third weaver and start triple weaving. (For instructions on triple weaving — also called three-rod wale — see Step 15, pages 26–27.) Weave three rounds between two spokes at a time, keeping the base of basket flat.

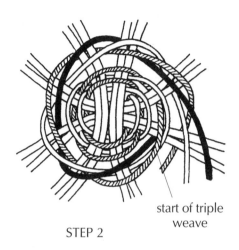

start of triple
weave

STEP 2

3. To make a very smooth transition to weaving between every spoke, do one round of triple weave with the spokes divided 1,1,2; 1,1,2; 1,1,2; and so on.

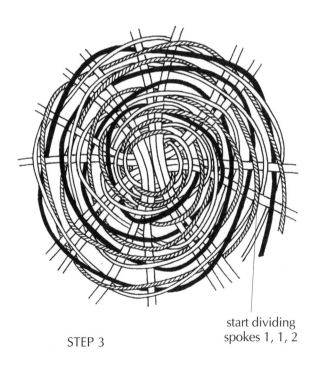

start dividing
spokes 1, 1, 2

STEP 3

4. Do one round of triple weave between each single spoke.

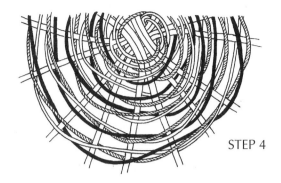

STEP 4

SHAPING THE SIDES

5. Hold the basket and gently bend the spokes upwards to form the sides. Weave four more rounds with vine rattan. Cut off the weavers and lay the ends to the inside of the basket.

6. Continue triple weaving in the established pattern, now using three horsetail rushes. Complete four rounds. Do not tug on these, but do pack the sides of the basket down firmly with fingers spread between the spokes, as in Step 5, page 5). The diameter of your basket should now measure approximately 8 inches.

7. Cut off the horsetail rush, change to vine rattan, and triple weave for two rounds. Do not allow the basket to grow any wider.

8. Change back to horsetail, and start to shape the basket inward. Continue to pack down the sides to keep weaving firm. Weave five rounds of triple weave.

9. Drop one weaver and twine (two weavers between single spokes) until the basket opening is the size you want. (The one shown on the front cover is 4 inches). Cut off the ends of the weavers and tuck them inside.

CREATING THE BORDER

10. Sharpen the ends of the sixteen 8-inch bye stakes, and push one down alongside each existing spoke. (Note: This is a decorative touch; it is not necessary for the structure of the basket.)

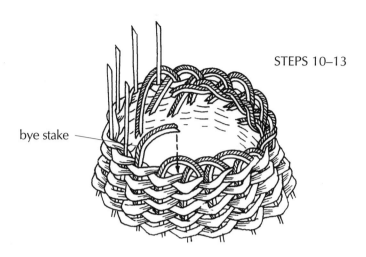

STEPS 10–13

bye stake

11. Trim all spokes to 5 inches.

12. Take one pair of spokes, bend them in front of the pair of spokes immediately on their right, and behind the pair to the right of that one, letting them lie on the inside of the basket. Continue in a counterclockwise direction all the way around. (This is just as in Steps 10 and 11, page 6, except that spokes are doubled.)

13. Repeat Step 12 for a second round, aiming the ends downward to create an inner rim. Trim off the ends.

LEVELING THE BASE

If the basket does not sit flat, soak the base for two minutes, and then push it in with your thumbs until it is slightly concave.

WILLOW WEAVES
SANDY WHALEN

 othing is prettier to me than blue-green waves of basket willow swaying in the wind. The following metaphor, which is my artistic statement, expresses my attitude toward my materials and work: "I think of my basketry as my own book: growing willow is my Dedication; harvesting and sorting becomes my Prologue; my baskets, lovingly created, are the Chapters in my book. Each basket portrays something new I've learned — a fresh idea or different experience. Like the proverbial novel that never quite gets finished, I hope to keep adding chapters."

The very word *willow* conjures up antiquity. Easy to grow and adaptable to almost any region or climate, willow (*Salix* spp.) has been used as a basket-weaving material since the earliest times. One can imagine willow being right at home in a North American Indian setting, in a medieval English village, even back to our hunter-gatherer ancestors — and rightly so. The ancient Romans considered willow to be one of the most useful of cultivated plants. They wove the smaller shoots into containers for household and personal belongings; they created heavier baskets for field and garden use. It was useful for everything from beehives to barnyard fences and crude shelters for the animals. There is even mention of willow being bent, covered with hides, and embossed with brass to make a very lightweight but durable shield for the soldiers.

In addition to the structural uses of the branches, the bark of some willows was brewed to make a comforting, although bitter tea, reputed to alleviate headaches — even before the time of the Romans. The medicinal component of willow can be identified as *salicin*, a precursor of salicylic acid, which is an ingredient in aspirin.

Willow was firmly established as a basket-weaving material in Europe when the first settlers came to North America. The

Europeans used a stake-and-strand method, in which a base is woven as a separate piece into which side spokes are subsequently pushed. Colonists brought basket-willow shoots with them to propagate, and the willow industry flourished from Colonial times until just after the Civil War.

There is evidence that the North American Indians also used willow. Their weaving style, however, was different from that of the Europeans. The Pacific Northwest Indians used very fine willow twigs as spokes and covered them with split bark or roots using a twining method. In the Southwest, Indians used willow as a core material for their coiled baskets.

Willow continues to be an amazing and versatile plant, well suited to most basketry needs. Let's look at how you can gather willow from the wild or grow your own.

RECOGNIZING WILLOW

When I first learned I might find willow growing wild, I thought to myself that it must be down South or elsewhere — not around here in Michigan. I certainly had never encountered it anywhere. Once I learned to recognize the plant, however, I was amazed at how prolific and abundant it really was.

Look for a grove, a thicket, or dense clump of rather scrublike bushes growing anywhere from 3 to 8 feet tall — about the size of a young clump of lilac bushes. From a distance, willow has an almost moundlike appearance and a characteristic silvery green color. Because it very often grows right along the roadside, it has earned the nickname "ditch willow." On closer inspection, you will recognize the typical long, slender willow leaves with a silvery underside on finely branched growth.

If you can identify a weeping willow tree, you will notice that the leaves of the wild willow are basically the same shape, size, and light green color, although perhaps a little more silver or gray. You may be curious about whether you can use the lovely long, slender, trailing branches of weeping willow. Some basket makers do use them, but it has been my experience that weeping willow becomes very brittle in a short time and thus produces a fragile and easily damaged basket. I prefer not to use it, therefore, and mention it only for leaf identification purposes.

Willow (*Salix* sp.)

HARVESTING WILLOW

From an uncared-for willow grove, you may be able to use some of the slender side branches, but these probably won't be very long. To cultivate a willow stand, so that it will be of most use to you, cut down a portion of the thicket almost to ground level (approximately 2 to 3 inches high) in the early spring to encourage long and slender one-year growth. You needn't worry about killing the plant, as you'll be assured by anyone who has had the experience of cutting down an unwanted tree, only to have stout one-year-old shoots sprout from the cut-off trunk the following spring. Severe pruning actually incites vigorous new growth.

Once you become a "willow watcher," you will observe that all willow, whether tree or shrub, is the very first plant to leaf out in the spring. Rods (branches — also called **withies** or **withes**) picked in early summer are still too immature and green for harvesting. They won't achieve the attractive reddish brown coloration of fall-harvested rods; in fact, summer-harvested rods usually turn black. Just as it is the first to leaf out, it is also the last to lose its leaves in the fall. Because the job of removing the leaves from the rod is extremely time consuming, it's nice if you can let Mother Nature do it for you. This makes the ideal harvest time late fall, after a few hard frosts have at least loosened the leaves, if not caused them to fall. Harvesting can continue from autumn into winter, as long as you don't mind the cold and your gloved hand can still hold on to the pruning shears. Be sure, however, to cut the rods *before* the sap begins to rise in the spring and the buds leaf out. This could be as early as the beginning of March, with snow still on the ground. (The exception to this is if you plan to peel the rod, a procedure described on page 20.)

Look for long, slender, unbranched rods. The standard rule is to choose rods no bigger than a pencil thickness. Anything much heavier will be too difficult to weave.

Parrot-beak pruning shears with a curved blade make cutting easy, as they don't slip off the round rods. Take cord or string to tie the willow in bundles for ease in transporting home.

SORTING AND STORING WILLOW

Once you get home, strip any remaining leaves from the rods, and place the rods in a tall bucket or wastebasket. English willow workers bury a 50-gallon drum in the floor of the sorting shed. They insert a measuring board marked in foot lengths into the drum along with the bundles of willow. They withdraw all the rods at 6 feet and above and place them in a pile. Next, they sort out all the 5-feet and above willow rods and put them in another pile. Four-foot rods come next, followed by 3-foot and sometimes 2-foot pieces. If you don't have a large volume of willow, you might want to withdraw the rods in half-foot increments. For example, place any rods 4 to 4½ feet in one group and 3½- to 4-foot rods in another group, right down to the shortest tips. Once everything is sorted, tie up the bundles.

With willow, the length usually determines the diameter of the rod. Six-foot rods are the stoutest and thickest; 3-foot rods are the most pliable and slender. I have on occasion cut off a 3-foot tip section of a heavier rod and used it, but it is never as pliable or "kind" as a rod that naturally grew to 3 feet.

Once you have your willow cut and sorted, you will probably be anxious to weave, but you should wait until the willow dries out and reaches its maximum shrinkage. I am aware that my opinion may differ from that of other willow weavers, but I *never* weave with green, or freshly harvested, rods. I always allow the willow to dry for at least two or three months before eventually soaking and mellowing it for weaving. It would be very difficult to get a tightly woven, sturdy basket if you used willow before it had completed its shrinking.

Store the sorted, tied willow bundles upright in a shed or garage or under an overhang where there is air circulation but protection from the rain.

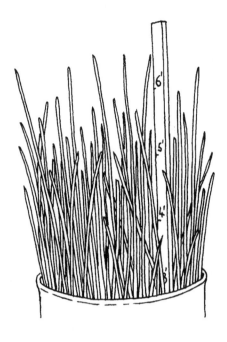

Willow-sorting barrel

GROWING YOUR OWN WILLOW

If you would like to grow your own stand of willow, you will find that it is a tenacious and easily grown plant. It is a misconception that it needs swampy, wet land in order to grow well. The fact is that it tolerates wet soil better than many plants and therefore can grow in almost any soil and climate.

Depending on your locality, cuttings should ideally be taken in January or February, before willow buds begin to swell and sap rises. This sometimes happens during those few warm spells that come and go before spring actually arrives. I cut 10-inch lengths of willow rod, about pencil size in diameter. From one 4-foot willow rod, I can usually cut three or four 10-inch sections before reaching the weak tip end. The tips can be prepared for use in weaving or simply discarded. I place the cuttings in an unsealed plastic bag, and put them somewhere cool, but protected from freezing.

I plant as soon as the soil can be worked in the spring, pushing each cutting into the ground, with at least two buds above the soil. I allow 10 to 12 inches between cuttings in rows approximately 2 feet apart. This tight planting forces the willow to grow tall and slender, as it reaches for the light.

It is very important to keep weeds from growing and competing with the willow the first few years. This is best accomplished by mulching with grass clippings, black plastic, or straw. (Avoid hay, which may harbor unwanted weed seeds.) Weeds are not as much of a problem in older, established willow beds, since the plants shade the weeds out.

First-year growth can be quite branchy, but the growth pattern usually improves in following years as the plant matures. I cut the willow to ground level in the fall, winter, or very early spring. I sometimes use the cut rods for weaving, or I may treat them as cuttings to increase the size of my willow bed the following spring.

Second- and third-year growth is straighter and taller. As the plant matures, it yields a greater number of shoots per plant. It takes at least three years to get a good strong stand of usable willow.

Whether the willow is usable or not, I cut it down each year. The plant begins to form a *stool* (stump), with multiple shoots appearing every spring. My old established willows have stumps that are bushel-basket size and rise 2 to 3 inches above ground. These plants produce hundreds of shoots every spring. (For additional information on growing willow, see pages 119–20.)

PREPARATION FOR WEAVING

Most people weave with the bark on the rod. The various colors are pleasing, and the rods need no additional preparation other than soaking. If you prefer peeled willow, however, you can do it

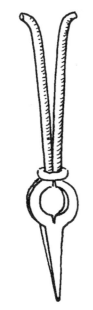

Traditional willow brake

Homemade willow brake

by one of two methods. One way is to place the fall-harvested rods in several inches of water, which keeps them alive until early spring when the sap rises. When the buds break, the bark no longer adheres to the rod, and it can be pulled off with a **willow brake.** This tool consists of two metal prongs arranged in a V shape. The rods are pulled through the V one by one, stripping the bark away. You can improvise a brake by driving two long spikes into a log and angling them to form the required V. This process produces a white willow rod. Whites can also be obtained by cutting the willow in the field, just as the buds begin to break, and peeling off the bark immediately. The bark loosens only as the sap rises and the plant is leafing out, and the time during which this occurs is limited.

Another way to remove the bark is to boil the willow in a large tank or trough until the bark comes off easily — usually six to nine hours, depending on the size of the rods. This may be done at any time. The first time I tried this, I used a livestock watering tank, with propane heaters for my heat source. It was very difficult to get that volume of water up to temperature, however, let alone boil. Subsequently, I have used a wood fire, which I prefer. The natural tannins that are released from the bark produce a soft dye, which gives the stripped willow rods a warm tan or buff color. Different varieties of willow produce different shades of buff.

After stripping the bark, no matter by which method, dry and store rods until ready to use.

When the time comes for weaving, the willow rods must be in a dampened and **mellowed** condition. After they have been soaked for a period of time in cold or warm water, they are wrapped in a damp towel and allowed to mellow, or rest, for several hours, preferably overnight. Here is a rough guide for how long to soak your willow:

Bark Rods		**Peeled Rods (white or buff)**	
3–4 feet	2–3 days	3–4 feet	½–1 hour
5–6 feet	3–4 days	5–6 feet	1–2 hours

Finding a place to soak bulky rods can be a problem. You're lucky if you have a stream or pond to soak them in. If you use the bathtub and the soaking requires three or four days, the kids can get very dirty! The best solution I've come up with is to use PVC pipe, available in hardware or plumbing supply stores. I buy a 4-inch diameter, 10-foot length of pipe, cut it in half to make two 5-foot soaking tubes, and seal one end of each tube with a cap so that I can stand the tubes on end. One tube requires only a bucket or so of water, yet holds enough willow for a big basket. Willow rods will float, so it is necessary to weight them no matter what method you use to soak them. A rag stuffed into the top of the tubes will keep the rods submerged.

I have found that a capful or so of fabric softener keeps the water fresh. It also seems to make the willow a little easier to handle.

TOOLS FOR WILLOW WORK

Willow does not require fancy tools, and you probably already have almost everything you will need:

Utility knife or jackknife

Parrot-beak pruners or diagonal cutters

Ice pick, awl, or bodkin

Cloth tape measure

Clip-type clothespins

Masking tape

String

Rapping iron (for example a small hammer, a
short narrow length of pipe, or other slender
tool that is heavy enough to beat
the weaving down)

Basket weight (for example: an old flat iron,
machine gear, lead weight, or rock; the weight
needs to be heavy but small enough to fit inside
the basket and hold it down while you weave)

With your tools assembled and the mellowed willow wrapped snugly in the damp towel on the floor beside you, you're ready to begin.

MATERIALS

BASE

Heavy willow: six 9" rods (spokes)

Very slim willow: four rods, at least 12" long (weavers)

Slim willow in a different bark color, buff, or white: six rods, at least 30" long (weavers)

Slim willow: four rods, at least 30" long (weavers)

SIDE SPOKES

Heavy willow: forty-eight 3' rods

BOTTOM AND TOP WALE

Slim willow: Twenty-four 3' rods (weavers)

OPENWORK WILLOW BOWL
12" diameter x 5¾" high

This openwork basket (shown on color page 88) is a good introduction to some traditional willow weaving techniques.

CREATING THE BASE

The six 9-inch-long spokes for the base should be of even thickness. When you place them, alternate tip and butt ends to keep spokes in balance.

1. With your bodkin or awl, puncture one of the base spokes at the exact center. Push the spoke onto the awl, and puncture the second and then the third spokes in the same manner. The spokes will split, and that's okay, because you are creating space to thread the other three base spokes through.

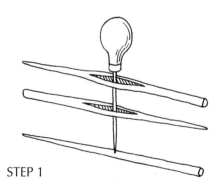

STEP 1

2. Thread the other three spokes into the "pocket" made by the awl. If you have difficulty getting a spoke in, cut a point at the end and give the spoke a twist as you insert it.

3. Begin a twine or pairing weave by inserting the tips of two of the very slim weavers into the "pocket"; pull the tips through so that they extend several inches beyond the opening. These ends will be secured as the weaving progresses. The long ends are the weavers. Take one of the weavers under a group of three spokes, and bring it out to the front. Bring the other weaver over the same group of three and take it to the back behind the next group of three and out to the front. Continue in this manner (called twining) twice around the groups of three, bringing the weavers to the top, and always using the left-hand weaver first.

4. Begin to separate the base spokes by continuing the twining, but now weaving over one spoke at a time, instead of the groups of three. To separate the base spokes, push each weaver down firmly on both sides of the spokes. This helps to keep the base weaving tight to the center.

5. When you reach the butt ends of your first two weavers, splice in the butt ends of two new weavers. Replace the left-hand one first, placing the butt end of the new weaver under the spoke and to the right of the old weaver for about ½ inch, as shown. Repeat with the other weaver. This saying may help you remember the splicing technique: "The old butt end comes toward me, the new butt end goes away." Try to keep the two ends as flat as possible at the splice. Make the second splice, and then continue to twine out to tips of the weavers. Always splice butt ends to butt ends and tip ends to tip ends. Weave about five rounds.

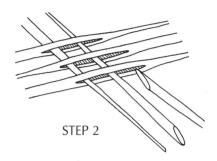

STEP 2

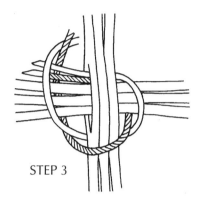

STEP 3

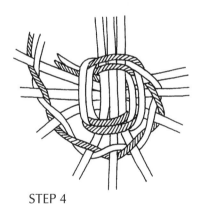

STEP 4

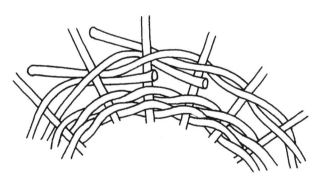

STEP 5

6. Use the six slim, contrasting weavers to weave a modified *French Rand.* Using two weavers at a time, you will be weaving to the right but placing the butt ends to the left. Beginning anywhere, place a butt end (A) under a spoke. Weaving to the right, go over one spoke, under the next, and back out to the front. Weave this weaver over and under one more time, just to hold it in place.

Start another weaver, placing the butt end (B) one spoke to the left of the spoke where you began the first weaver. As before, weave over and under, and over and under again to hold this weaver in place.

Skip two base spokes to the left and start another weaver (C) under the next spoke, exactly as before. Begin a fourth weaver (D) with the butt end one spoke to the left of the third weaver. You may want to weave these two until you get to the spokes where the first two rods began.

Skip two more base spokes to the left, and add another pair of spokes (E and F) at the next two spokes. Be sure to place the last two weavers right next to the center twining and *not* over any of the modified French Rand weavers. Weave until you get to the previously placed weavers — but *do not overtake them.*

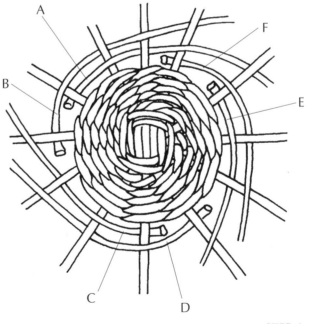

STEP 6

7. With all six weavers now in place, weave around the base in simple over and under **randing** (weaving). Take care never to overtake the previous weavers. Weave each in succession, out to their tips. Use clip clothespins to secure the tips before you do the final twine. This section of randing will be about 1 inch wide.

8. Use the four remaining slim weavers to complete the base. Use the same twine weave that you used in Steps 3–5. Begin this section with two tips, weave to the butts, splice in two weavers at the butt ends, and weave to their tips. The completed base should measure about 7 inches across.

EXTRA WEAVERS

If you need to add extra weavers to obtain the desired base dimensions, you will need to add two "sets" in order to end in tips. Sometimes the splices tend to be all on one side of the base. If this happens, plan the tip placement so the splices will be in different sections of the base.

SIDE SPOKES

9. Select twenty-four of the side spokes. In order to have spokes as consistent as possible in diameter, note the thickness of one rod about 5 or 6 inches above its butt end. Hold several other rods in your hand, and comparing them to the first rod, slide them up or down until they closely match the first rod. Trim them off as necessary at the heavier butt ends. Be careful not to cut any rods shorter than 24 inches; you may have to accept a slightly heavier rod so as not to cut a rod too short.

10. Now you must **slype** the end (as the English would say) — meaning, make a point on the end of each rod by trimming it on an angle with scissors or a knife.

11. Trim off three or four of the base spokes even with the base weaving. Insert the side spokes created in Step 10 on each side of these base spokes. Let the pointed end of the rod slide alongside the base spoke, and push it into the base as far as possible. Trim

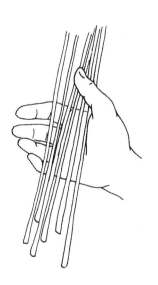

STEP 9

off another three or four base spokes, and continue inserting side spokes into the base until all twenty-four have been used. (See drawing, Step 12.)

12. You will now *prick up* the spokes by puncturing them with your knife right where you want them to bend at the base. Pricking up takes the tension off the spoke and keeps the spokes from cracking when bent, leaving a smooth bend on the outside. Take care not to go completely through the spoke with your knife. Place the point of the knife against the spoke, pull the spoke up as you twist the knife, and then let the spoke relax. Go all around the basket in this manner.

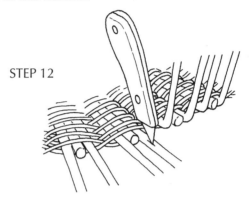

STEP 12

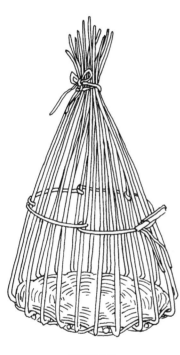

STEP 13

13. Weight the basket down. Temporarily tie up the tips in a bundle to keep them out of the way. Take another piece of string, about 4 feet long, and attach one end halfway up one of the side spokes with a clothespin. Skip about four spokes, and loop the string around the next spoke. Skip three or four more spokes and again loop the string around the next one, and so on, until you reach the spoke where you began. Remove the clothespin, and tie the ends of the string in a bow. Remove the temporary tie at the top. Examine the basket framework, and either tighten or loosen the string to get the desire flare. The looped string can easily be raised or lowered.

14. Work on the skeleton of the basket. Straighten spokes where necessary; bend any kinks out. This skeleton should look good before you even start weaving.

BOTTOM WALE (THREE-ROD)

15. You will need twelve of the slim weavers for this step. Choose them according to their heights, since the shortest one will stop the wale. Select three. Beginning with tips, place each one under an upright spoke. Take the far left-hand weaver (A) first, and, weaving to the right, weave over two uprights, under one, and out to the front. Again, take the far left-hand weaver (B), go over two, under one, and out to the front. Continue in this manner until you reach the butt ends of all three weavers. This over two, under one weave is also known as a *triple weave.*

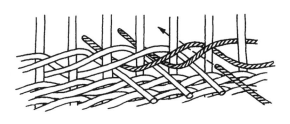

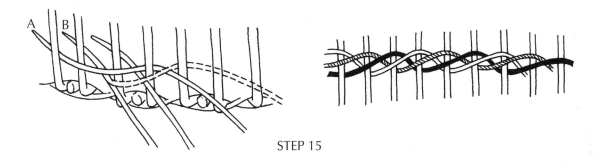

STEP 15

16. When you reach the butt ends, splice in three new butt ends and continue the wale.

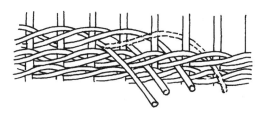

STEP 16

17. When you reach the tips, lock them in by following the weave pattern and pulling them through to the outside.

STEP 17

RAPPING DOWN

Be sure to rap the weaving down periodically to keep everything nice and tight. The wale is a strong weave. Your goal should be to get control of the direction of the basket, so that the spokes are evenly spaced all around.

ADDITIONAL SIDE SPOKES

18. Take the remaining twenty-four spokes for the side spokes, and even them up and trim them, as in Step 9. Slype each one, as in Step 10.

19. In between each upright spoke, the weaving you just completed will have created a "wale pocket." Push the pointed end of one of the spokes down into each of these pockets. Take care not to push the tips beyond the base.

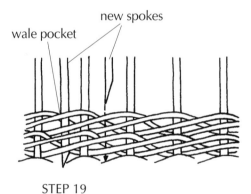

STEP 19

20. Remove the string. At this point, it is probably more bothersome than helpful.

TOP WALE

21. Begin the top wale with tips, the same as for the base. Since there is nothing to rest the tips on, I tape the tips to the uprights with a small piece of masking tape to hold them securely. Tape each tip exactly the same distance above the bottom wale. For the basket on page 88, I taped the tips 3½ inches above the wale. (For purposes of illustration, these are shown on a downward angle. Actual weaving should proceed parallel to bottom wale, 3½ inches above it.)

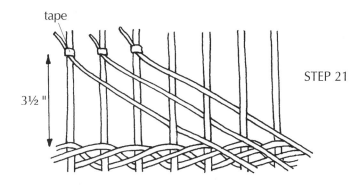

STEP 21

22. Weave the three-rod wale as in Step 15 (over two, under one). Since the sides are open, you will need to add another group of tips, directly opposite the first set, to help keep the weaving even. With these tips, do a chase weave in the following manner: After weaving through a few spokes with the first group of three, start the second set directly opposite. Tape the tips as in Step 21. Weave those three for a few spokes, and then go back to the original three and weave over the second set. Never allow the second group to overtake the first group. Weave these alternate groups out to their butt ends; they should end on opposite sides of the basket. Splice in three butt ends on each side, and continue the wale out to the tips of the weavers. Try to keep the weaving as tight as possible. It is also very important to have the top of the basket as even as possible before you create the border. Using a ruler, either rap up on the underside of the wale weaving or rap down on its top.

TRAC BORDER

23. To make the border, you will need a thin board or a wood or plastic ruler 1¼ inches wide (I used a *spoke weight*). Use this as a guide to bend each of the spokes exactly 1¼ inches from the top of the wale — the necessary height for this particular border. Be very careful to keep the spokes straight and upright — not slanted in either direction — at the point of the elbow bend.

24. To make a trac border, begin with any spoke. Using the spoke itself, weave over two, under two, over one, under one, over one, under one, and out to the outside of the basket. Weave to the right and down toward the wale. Repeat with each new spoke to the right. With each pass you will travel eight spokes altogether. Keep a straight angle as you weave down to the wale. You may occasionally want to rap the weaving down. Each spoke should bend where you kinked it in Step 23.

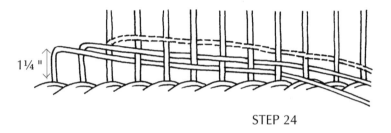

1¼ "

STEP 24

25. When you get to the last several upright spokes, weave them through the already-woven border, carefully following the established pattern out to the end.

26. Trim all the ends.

27. Turn the basket upside down, and rap the bottom of the wale tightly to the border.

WILD WILLOW-WARE

10" diameter x 3¾" high
(not including handle)

*Sturdy and practical, this basket with a handle
(shown on color page 88) is one you will
enjoy using or offering as a gift.*

BASE

The six 9-inch base spokes should be uniform. When you arrange them for the base, alternate tip and butt ends in order to have an even thickness to the base.

1. Split three spokes and thread three other spokes through as in Steps 1–2 on pages 22–23.

2. Twine the base as in Steps 3–5 on page 23. It is not necessary to do a modified French Rand for this basket; you may simply twine the whole base. Be sure, however, to end with tips. The base should be approximately 7½ inches in diameter.

BASE

Heavy willow: six 9" rods
(spokes)

Very slim willow: four rods,
at least 12" (weavers)

Slim willow in a different
bark color, buff, or white:
six rods, about 24" (weavers)

Slim willow: four rods, at
least 30" (weavers)

TOP WALE (OPTIONAL)

Willow: twelve rods, about
3' (weavers)

SIDE SPOKES

Fairly heavy willow: twenty-
four 3' rods (side spokes)

FOOT BORDER AND SIDE

Slim, flexible willow:
twenty-four rods, at least
28"–30" (weavers)

HANDLE

Heavy willow bow: about
30" (handle)

Medium willow: eight rods,
at least 1½-2 times the
length of the handle (for
wrapping)

SIDE SPOKES

3. Slype the twenty-four 3-foot side spokes, and insert them into each side of the base spokes as in Steps 10–11 on pages 25–26.

4. Prick up around the base as in Step 12, page 26. Temporarily tie the tips together in a bundle to keep them out of your way. ·

FOOT BORDER AND SIDE WEAVE

5. Slype the remaining twenty-four 3-foot spokes (border spokes), and insert two between each two upright spokes, as shown. Those added in this step will form the foot border and then continue as side weavers.

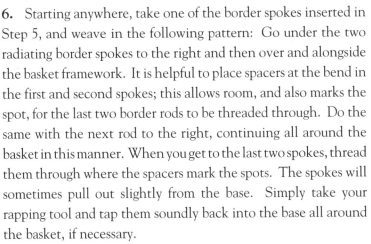

STEP 5

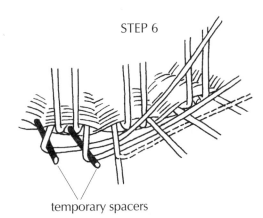

STEP 6

temporary spacers

6. Starting anywhere, take one of the border spokes inserted in Step 5, and weave in the following pattern: Go under the two radiating border spokes to the right and then over and alongside the basket framework. It is helpful to place spacers at the bend in the first and second spokes; this allows room, and also marks the spot, for the last two border rods to be threaded through. Do the same with the next rod to the right, continuing all around the basket in this manner. When you get to the last two spokes, thread them through where the spacers mark the spots. The spokes will sometimes pull out slightly from the base. Simply take your rapping tool and tap them soundly back into the base all around the basket, if necessary.

Hint: I invariably stand when doing this and hold the basket upside down. The weave is the same, except that you will be weaving over, instead of under, the first two rods. I chant to myself as I work: "Over two and up alongside of the basket — over two and up alongside of the basket" and so on.

SIDE WEAVING

7. The twenty-four border spokes are now in place to serve as weavers around the twenty-four side spokes. The weave for the sides is a French Rand, in a continuation of the over two, under one pattern of the foot border. Weight the basket down, and re-tie the upright spokes. Realign the side spokes, which have probably gotten out of order with the pull and tug of weaving the foot border. You will be weaving to the right.

8. You will need three clip-type clothespins to serve as markers. Beginning anywhere (as at A), go over two spokes, under one, and come out to the front, covering the spoke that already lies in that space. Clip these two spokes together as a pair.

Take the next spoke to the *left* of the first weaver (B). Go over two uprights, under one, and out to the front. Again, clip the spoke with which you have just woven to the spoke that shares the space between uprights. Repeat for the third pair (C). (Leave the clothespins in place; you will not need them again until you have completed the round.)

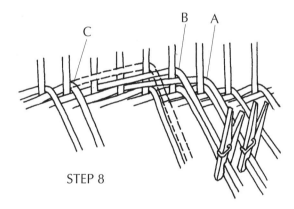

STEP 8

Hint: The weaving spokes may not line up absolutely true until the next round, but you will weave accurately if you always bring the active spoke out to the left of the one just used.

9. Continue around the basket to the left, weaving each spoke over two and under one to the right, and coming through to the front. Stop when you reach the first pair clipped together. The clothespin markers are reminders that the top rod has been woven but *not* the bottom one. Keeping the top spoke up and out of the way, weave the bottom one over two, under one, and out to the front.

Go to the left and remove the next clothespin. Keeping *both* top spokes up and out of the way, weave the bottom one over two, under one, and out to the front.

Remove the last clothespin. Keeping all three previously woven top rods up and out of the way, weave the bottom spoke, over two, under one, and out to the front. This finishes one round.

10. Pound all the weavers down snugly. All clothespins have been removed. If done correctly, you should have a spoke extending from behind each upright.

11. Begin round two anywhere you want. Weave it in the same way as the first round. If you have trouble finding the spoke that should be paired with the weaver, try this: as you bring the weaver down and out to the front, mentally block out all the other willow spokes *except* the two spokes that are within the two uprights the weaver is coming through — the weaver and the one already in place. That's the pair to mark. It's easy to illustrate this on paper, but when you are actually weaving, the spokes may go off in odd directions, and it's easy to get confused.

Advance left around the basket until you get back to the clothespin markers. When you remove the pins in order to weave, be sure to lift the top spokes and weave only the bottom ones.

12. Continue in the same manner with additional rounds, marking the first three pairs each time. Weave out to tips. When the shortest one is used up, the weave ends.

13. Pound down the weaving to make the basket level. Check the height with a ruler to be sure it measures the same all the way around. If you desire additional height, you can top the weaving with several rounds of waling, as in Steps 15–17, pages 26–27. As mentioned, a wale is a good weave to use to bring your basket under control — if it's flaring outward too much, for instance, or the uprights need straightening.

THREE-ROD BORDER: BEND DOWN

This is a simple but sturdy border, frequently used by willow weavers. It has the same thickness as the side weaving. There are four-, five-, and six-rod borders; the greater the number of rods, the thicker the border. The method is the same for each, however, and the principles learned here can be applied to any rod border.

To keep the weaving pattern clear in my mind, I like to break the rod border process down into four parts: (1) the bend down; (2) making pairs; (3) leaving a spoke; (4) threading through.

14. Starting anywhere, bend four uprights at a point ⅜ to ½ inch above the end of the weaving. The width of a clip clothespin makes a good gauge for the bend. The number of uprights bent down is always the number of the border plus one for good measure. For example, a three-rod border requires four bends; a four-rod border requires five bends, and so on. The bend allows room for threading through later on. After this bending, or kinking, process, allow the uprights to go back to their original position.

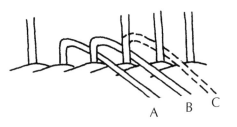

STEP 14

15. With the first bent-down upright on the left (A), go behind the upright to its right and out to the front. With the next upright (B), go behind the one to its right and out to the front. Repeat with the next upright (C). You now have three uprights extending out from the basket.

THREE-ROD BORDER: MAKING PAIRS

16. With the first upright used in Step 15 (A), go over the next two — the first one you go in front of is bent down, but should be counted — and then under one and out to the front. Now, take the first (still unused) upright on the left (B), bring it behind the upright to its right, and lay it alongside and just to the right of the upright just put there.

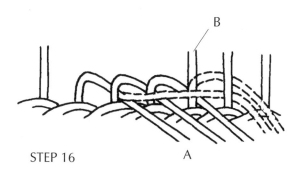

STEP 16

This is the first pair. Make the second and third pairs in the same way. You now have three pairs extending from the side of the basket. Try to keep these pairs as flat as possible; it's important you don't get them twisted. The upright last bent down should always be on the right.

THREE-ROD BORDER: LEAVING A SPOKE

In this step you will be leaving a spoke (and breaking up the pair) and making a new pair on the right all the way around the basket. The weave remains the same — over two, under one, and out to the front.

17. Count backwards from the right to the far left pair. This is the pair you are going to break up. It's very obvious at this point which pair to take, but I recommend that beginners do this counting step in order to avoid confusion. Three pairs should always extend from the side.

18. Of the pair selected in Step 17, leave the left spoke, and take the spoke closer to the basket (A). Going toward the right, weave over two, under one, and out to the front. Take the first upright on the left (B), bring it down under the upright to its right, and lay it alongside and just to the right of the rod just placed there. This makes a new pair.

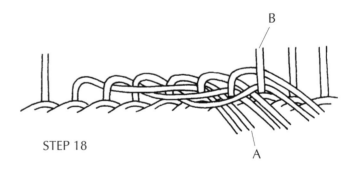

STEP 18

19. Count back three pairs. Repeat Step 18.

20. Continue in this pattern, dropping a spoke and making a new pair, until back to the start. Thread the last spoke (A) and, finally, the last upright (B) under the "elbow" (C) created in Step 14. You now have single spokes radiating around the basket, three pairs, and three places where there aren't any spokes. "Threading Through" will complete the border.

STEP 20

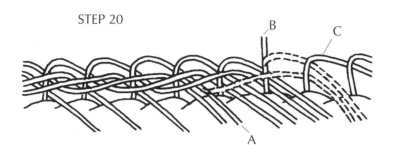

THREE-ROD BORDER: THREADING THROUGH

21. Starting at the point where there are no radiating spokes, count back three. Take the spoke closer to the basket (A), and bring it to the right over two bent down spokes. With your awl, *follow* the second bent-down spoke (B), and thread the active spoke through where the bent-down spoke meets or touches the elbow to its right (C). Push the awl through the space to make room to thread the spoke through. You now have a single spoke on the right and two pairs on the left.

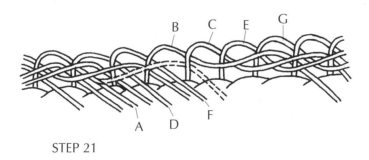

STEP 21

22. Working with the next pair, drop the left spoke, and take the one closer to the basket (D). As in Step 21, go over two, and use your awl to make space to thread the spoke through the next elbow (E). Note that in addition to going under the elbow, you must also go under one horizontal border spoke.

23. Take the remaining pair, drop the left one, take the one closer to the basket (F), go over two, and thread it through the next elbow (G) in the same manner. Note that besides the elbow, there are now *two* horizontal border spokes to go under. This finishes the border. You should now have one spoke coming from behind each spoke all around the basket.

24. Snug up all around by pulling each extended border spoke slightly out from the basket. As you pull, trim each off, and let it snap back even with the sides of the basket.

HANDLE BOW AND WRAPPING RODS

25. Gently bend the heavy willow bow you selected for a handle. Trim the larger end, and slype to a point.

26. At the point where you decide to place the handle, push your awl down through the border alongside the side spoke to make room. Remove the awl, and push the slyped end of the handle bow into that pocket. I try to push it down as far as I can — almost to the base, if possible.

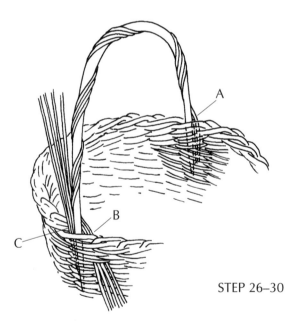

STEP 26–30

27. By eye, estimate where the other end of the handle bow should be placed. It needs to follow alongside of a side spoke. Place the unattached end outside the basket, and adjust the height of the handle up or down to get the arch you want. A good height is usually 6½ to 7 inches above the top of the basket, but this is a matter of personal preference. Assuming you can push the handle bow into the weaving at least halfway down the basket, trim off and slype the end, as required. Make a pocket with your awl, and push the second side of the handle rod home.

28. Slype the ends of four of the handle wrappers, and push them into the basket, to the left of the handle bow (at A); try to place them close to the handle so that they surround it as much as possible.

29. Working with these four as a unit, wrap them around the handle bow to the right. As you progress, leave enough space to accommodate a group of four rods coming from the opposite direction. It's best if you grab the tips and try to support the "loop" as you bring the rods around; avoid getting kinks in these rods, if at all possible. Depending on the flexibility and size of the rods, three wraps will usually take you to the other side. End with the rods on the *inside* of the basket (at B). Working from the inside, thread each rod through the weaving to the outside in the same sequence as they came around the bow. Thread them through to the outside at the space to the left (looking at the bow from the *inside* of the basket) of the handle bow, either between the last weaving and the top wale or about an inch or so down.

30. Slype the four remaining wrapping rods. On the opposite side from where you began in Step 28 (in other words, where you ended in Step 29), insert the four remaining wrapping rods through the weaving (at C). As in Step 28, place them to the left of the handle and behind it enough that they encircle it as much as possible. Bring them around the handle to fill in the space left by the first group. As before, grab the tips and ease the rods around the bow.

31. Thread these rods to the outside as described in Step 29. If there are gaps, you may add additional rods.

32. The ends of the four handle wrappers are now to the right at each end of the handle on the outside of the basket. Working on one side at a time, take the left-hand wrapper to the left, up behind the handle bow, and snug it up tightly as you bring it to the right and out to the front. Take it down across itself to the left, and thread it through to the inside, even with its point of exit on the right.

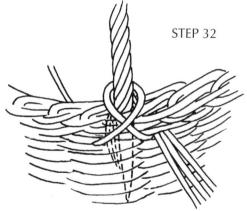

STEP 32

33. Do the same with the remaining wrapping rods, in sequence from the left. Always pull up tightly as you bring them around the bow. The remaining tips can be twisted up all together and woven away. Treat them as a single weaver, or take pairs and weave them in on each side of the handle. Trim off any remaining ends.

34. Repeat Steps 32–33 on the other side of the basket.

WEAVING WITH RED-OSIER DOGWOOD

MARYANNE GILLOOLY

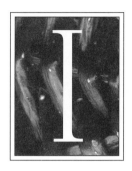 do not weave baskets exclusively with "wild" materials, but I always enjoy the instant gratification of collecting branches, vines, or grasses and sitting down to weave a basket in the warmth of the afternoon sun. What a pleasure — to weave my worries away in a basket. Whether I make a free-form vessel, a woven basket, or a simple wreath of looped branches, I consider the time well spent, no matter what I end up with when I am finished. The process itself becomes a sort of therapy. I know I have once again fed my soul and connected with nature.

Where I live in the Northeast, red-osier dogwood is a common sight. Its bright red branches, valued by basket weavers, appear in abundance in swampy pastures, wet areas, and along the roadsides. Although it is also appreciated for its flowers and fruit, its importance for basket makers is the rich burgundy-red color of its branches. In late spring, this dogwood bears flat clusters of tiny white flowers, which are followed by bluish white berries in later summer. In autumn, the leaves turn a russet red, and during winter, the bark on the bare red branches stands out vividly against the white snow.

The true red-osier dogwood (*Cornus sericea*) is an ornamental shrub. At a manageable mature height of about 6 feet, it is easy to harvest. This dogwood is also hardy enough to be heavily pruned. In fact, cutting not only helps the shrub to thrive, but it also encourages new growth, which in turn produces branches that are even brighter red in color. It grows in clumps and spreads by underground runners.

Other *Cornus* species also have wonderful red-colored branches. The young branches of Tartarian dogwood (*C. alba*) and the closely related Siberian dogwood (*C. alba* 'Siberica Variegata') turn red later in winter. C. *alba* grows higher than C. *sericea* (6–10 feet), and its branches are more red than burgundy. These varieties of dogwood are so closely related, however, that even botanists have difficulty telling them apart.

A very interesting golden-twig dogwood (C. *sericea* 'Flaviramea') has yellowish branches; its young twigs are even brighter yellow than the older growth.

All of these dogwoods are native to the North Temperate Zone, from Canada through New England, south to Virginia and west to Nebraska. In fact, you can find one kind or another in all parts of the U.S. except in California and the hottest southern states. You can propagate dogwood by taking cuttings of young growth in late spring or early summer or by digging up and replanting the underground runners that the true red-osier produces.

If the red-osier is not available in your area, you can make the projects in this chapter with branches from shrubs like pussy willow, forsythia, quince, or willow, or even from young saplings.

GATHERING RED OSIER

Late fall and winter are the best times to gather red-osier dogwood. The stems contain less moisture then and the shrub has lost its leaves — a real advantage, because you are spared the process of picking them off before weaving with the branches. In addition, the branches are at their brightest red and thus very easy to distinguish, especially if there is snow on the ground. The only difficulty can be the combination of cold weather and the swampy areas where it grows. Wear warm clothing and good boots!

I usually gather my red osier right along the roadsides. If road crews have cut down the dogwood the year before, you'll find lots of new shoots to collect. When collecting, look for this new, younger growth. These branches are brighter red and have smoother, straighter stems. The older branches are thicker and have rougher, brownish red bark. The older growth also branches out a lot at the top. I like to gather both old and new branches, however. The older, thicker branches are good for framework, and the newer, thinner ones are good to weave with.

Cut the branches as long as you can, so you have adequate pieces to work with. Be sure to cut them close to the ground or where they meet the main stem, as this is more healthful for the shrub.

PREPARATION OF MATERIALS

When collecting, I usually gather only what I need for a specific project and use the material within a few weeks of gathering. If the branches are stored in a cool, shady place, they will remain pliable enough to work with. Do not, however, let them get damp and mildewed.

The disadvantage of working with fresh materials is that the branches shrink when dry, and this causes the weaving to loosen in time. Because of this, you may want to dry the material first. When you have cut a good-sized bundle of branches, clip off any side branches, tie them up, and store them in a cool, dry place. Lay them flat on boards or a table, or place them upright in a barrel or can. You may want to keep the thinner, straighter ones separate from those that are thicker. This separation of weaving branches from framework pieces will make things more organized later, when you work with the materials.

Before using the dried branches, you must soak them until they are pliable and easy to use without breaking. Be careful, however, that the bark does not peel off. This seems more likely to happen when the twigs have been soaked too long. The bark also retains its color better if you soak it as little as possible.

Red-osier dogwood makes a strong and strikingly red-colored basket that mellows and darkens with age. Each basket is beautiful and unique. Working with this material, however, is always a challenge. Each twig of the dogwood is different — some rough, some smooth; some curved, some straight. None of them is perfect. You'll have to learn to let perfection go. Even, flat rows of weaving are impossible! This is a rough-textured, rustic basket made of natural, wild materials, but that is its charm. In spite of the imperfections, or maybe because of them, your basket will be unlike any other. What may seem like a rugged, rustic basket will actually be a true expression of *you*, who cut, collected, wove, and shaped a bit of nature.

Because the materials are uneven and irregular, they may also be a little awkward to handle. Use plenty of clothespins, as well as your strength, and exert your will. Try to get a feel for the material; work and play with it, and go with its flow. The flow may sometimes feel more like wrestling an alligator, but try to conquer it. Let the dogwood know who is boss.

Your equipment needs for working with red osier are minimal: garden clippers, needle-nose pliers, a few clip-type clothespins, and an awl.

ROUND RED-OSIER
DOGWOOD BASKET
12" diameter x 3½ " high

*The directions given below are for a basket 12 inches in diameter.
Depending on your needs and materials, you can make it in any size
you wish. Three different versions are shown on color page 89.*

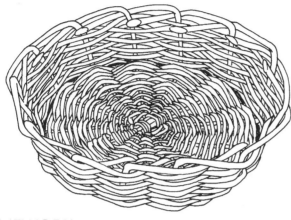

Thick red-osier dogwood:
seven 36" stems (spokes)

Thin red-osier dogwood:
eighteen long stems
(weavers)

FRAMEWORK

1. The framework for this basket starts with a crossed beginning.
Lay three of the thick stems (spokes) side by side, alternating the
thicker ends of the stems. Lay three more stems on top of the
others, crossing them in the center at right angles. Again,
alternate the thicker ends of the stems.

BASE

2. The first weaving will help to secure the six pieces of the
framework together and establish a strong beginning, so be sure to
keep these rows as tight and close together as you can. Start with
a long, very thin stem of dogwood. Place the thinner end of the
weaver under one of the top-most groups of spokes. Weave
clockwise over the first group of spokes, under the second, over
the third, and under the fourth. Tuck the end of the weaver in as
you continue to weave another row, ending under the fourth set
of spokes again.

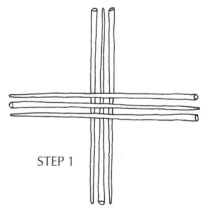

STEP 1

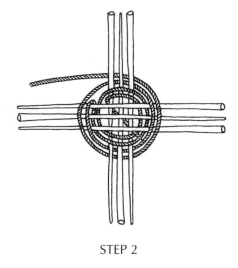

STEP 2

Bend the weaver, and wrap it all the way around the last set of spokes and weave two rows in the other direction. You have now completed four rows of weaving, two rows on each side of each group of three.

3. Flip the whole piece over so the regular over, under weaving can continue in a clockwise direction. (If you feel more comfortable weaving in a counterclockwise direction, do not reverse sides.) Separate the spokes and weave under one spoke, over the next until you reach the last spoke.

Cut the remaining thick stem piece to 18 inches. Make a good angled cut with scissors or clippers so it will fit snugly. Insert it into the weaving, next to the last group of spokes. This odd-numbered spoke makes it possible to have a continuous weave without having the weaver go under and over the same spoke on adjacent rows.

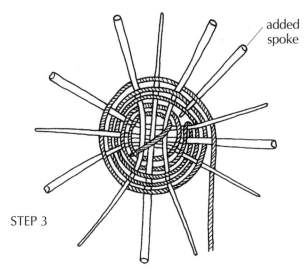

added spoke

STEP 3

4. Continue weaving over and under, including the new spoke. Spread the spokes, so they are spaced evenly apart. Weave as even and flat as you can until the bottom measures about 8 inches.

SIDES

Basket weavers often begin a simple twining or wale at this point in twig basketry (see pages 26–27), to help hold the spokes upright. Because the dogwood is a fairly thick material, however, I simply continue in an over, under weaving, as in the bottom of the basket.

This part of the weaving is difficult, because as you weave you must also force the spokes upward to form the sides of the basket. You can shape the basket any way you like. The sides can go up straight, flare out, or curve in. The baskets pictured on page 89 have straight sides, but you may want to play with the shape a little, or the branches may want to form their own shape. Sometimes you have to force the spokes of the basket into the shape or direction you want.

5. Turn the woven basket bottom upside down, if you wish the weaving to continue in a clockwise direction.

6. The spokes need to be *upset* (bent upward) to begin to form the sides of the basket. With the needle-nosed pliers, gently crimp each spoke at the edge of the last row of weaving. Be careful not to damage the bark. Ease each spoke into an upright position.

7. Weave in the established over, under pattern until the sides measure about 3 inches. (You can weave the basket higher, if you like. Just be sure to leave enough spoke (about 8 inches) to form the rim.

ADDING WEAVERS

When a weaver is used up, simply lay a new piece next to the old one. They should lie side by side for a few inches, over and under a few spokes, so both the new and the old ends stay in place. Use a clothespin to help hold the ends down while you weave a few rows to hold them in place. Alternate thick and thin ends of the weavers. For instance, if the old piece of dogwood ends at the thick part of the stem, start with the thin end of the new piece of dogwood.

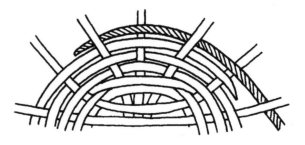

Adding a weaver

RIM

8. With the needle-nosed pliers, crimp the spokes near the last row of weaving. Crush the fibers just enough to help them bend without breaking. Rewet, if necessary.

9. Beginning with any spoke, bend it toward the right and bring it behind the next spoke and in front of the next. Next, bring it between that spoke and the next to the inside of the basket. (It will be trimmed later.) Weave each spoke to the right in turn and repeat.

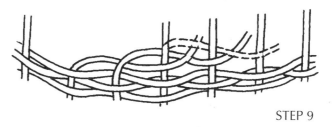

STEP 9

The last two spokes can be confusing because the spokes you need to weave through have already been woven down. Keep the pattern in mind, and weave behind the spoke to the right, in front of the next, already woven spoke, and tuck it underneath and between the next two woven spokes to the inside of the basket. For the last spoke, weave behind the spoke just woven, go under and through to the outside of the basket, in front of the next spoke, and tuck it under and through to the inside.

FINISHING

10. Trim all the ends of the rim pieces. (Do not cut them too short, however, or the rim will come apart.) Trim any long ends on weavers. If the basket doesn't sit evenly, you may need to pop up its bottom. Turn it upside down, and put some pressure on the bottom to flatten it or even make a depression in it. The basket should rest on the outside edges of the basket base.

11. I like to add a little interest to the basket by tucking in some of the leftover red-osier branches. You may wish to try other materials to create an interesting design element. Vines, birch bark, seed pods, branches, and grasses can all be used to embellish your basket.

VARIATIONS

Following the same process, you can make a little basket of the thinner side shoots, small branches, or leftover pieces from the original basket. Use the thinnest pieces for weavers, and make the spokes about a foot long and slightly thicker than the weavers.

If you would like to try a larger basket, just use thicker and longer stems. Remember that the framework must be larger, so you will need more spokes. Start out with the number of spokes used in the framework in Step 1, page 45. As you weave out from the center, the spaces between spokes will widen and you will have to add more. Cut new spokes on an angle and slide them into the weaving next to existing spokes. Keep the total number of spokes uneven so that the weaving remains under, over throughout. It is best to add extra spokes *before* beginning the side weaving.

RED-OSIER DOGWOOD WREATH

12" diameter

*This wreath (shown on color page 89) is made
with some of the thicker, branching twigs of the dogwood.*

Good-size red-osier
branches: six pieces

Medium-size red-osier with
branching tops: six pieces

Raffia

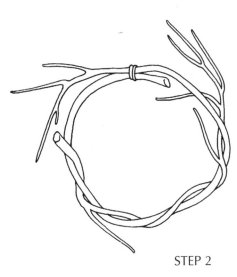

STEP 2

1. Take the longest branch, and curve it into a circle. Use raffia or string to tie it together.

2. Add another branch by laying its end under the foundation circle you made in Step 1. Bring it through the center and around the foundation several times. Leave the branching ends sticking out. Add as many branches as you like, spacing the top, branching parts evenly around the wreath. Don't worry about being completely symmetrical, however; let the shapes of the twigs help you to determine the shape of the wreath. These wreaths are much more interesting if they are irregularly shaped. My wreath (shown on page 89) is fairly thin and light, but you may need something with more bulk, depending on where it will be hung.

3. Form a hanger by tying a loop in an end of the raffia you used to tie the branches together.

4. Add pieces of dried magnolia, hydrangea, roses from your garden, or whatever you have available. Wire or glue them in place, or simply tuck them in between the branches.

ALL WRAPPED UP IN DIFFERENT SHAPES

NANCY BASKET

 atural basketry roots us in a tradition of seeking the wisdom of the plant kingdom. The Native American legend of the animals' and plants' councils suggests that it is time to remember the old ways, to ask the plants for the cures they hold, to believe the answers they give, and, to the best of one's ability, to act accordingly. Many who make or collect baskets do so because of an inner need to bond again with the earth. For me, gathering my own materials from field or garden helps me remember the time, effort, and skill necessary to build a basket; allows me to touch our mother, Earth; and helps relieve stress. I gather my basketry materials by hand in the respectful

WHY THE PLANTS BECAME HUMANITY'S HELPERS

"Long time ago," the animals came together in their respective tribal councils. They were angry that humanity was no longer showing them any respect or consideration. Hunters killed for sport; others killed just because they were afraid of the animals. The animals decided to give the two-leggeds diseases of all kinds to pay them back for their thoughtlessness.

The plants, on the other hand, had no such complaints against humans, and so they decided in their council to help the humans overcome the diseases wrought upon them by the animals. The plants knew that all things must remain in balance. The two-leggeds simply needed to ask a plant for its wisdom, and the cure would be available to the seeker.

tradition of Native Americans. When we take, we give back —
a gift of tobacco, hair from our heads, beads, money — anything
we value. In this way, we remember that we are all of one family,
just of different tribes.

My path — that of the Red Road and the peaceful warrior —
has led me to live in many different parts of the United States and
Canada, and my basketry has been influenced by my experiences
with many places and people. In addition, my baskets have their
origins in the traditions of three of the Four Tribes of Humanity
— Red, Black, White, and Yellow. From the ancient traditions
of the Red Tribe come my Native American baskets of various
indigenous materials. From the Black Tribe, come my Gullah-
Afro baskets of South Carolina sweet grass. From the White
Tribe, my German rye-straw baskets. My specialty, pine-needle
baskets, encompasses all these traditions and celebrates the sim-
ilarities in all the tribes.

Many of my baskets represent typical White Tribe work, in
both form and function. Others, such as the cradleboard and
effigy baskets, are ancient "remembered" designs — those designs
that relate to ancient tradition, but of which no historical exam-
ples have been catalogued. For instance, archaeologists recently
discovered 3,000-year-old coiled basketry fragments in rock caves
in Arkansas. This dates them to a time long before the removal
of the Southeastern tribes along the infamous Trail of Tears.
Authorities agree that, in all likelihood, ancient Cherokee basket
makers used the long pine needles that grew in southern areas for
their baskets. Even today, basket makers of the Alabama Coushatti tribe and some Cherokee basket makers coil pine-needle
effigy baskets, cradle boards, and other basket shapes. I feel that
some of the designs of my coiled long-needle pine baskets are
"remembered" from this ancient tradition.

Native American basket makers use distinctive family designs that distinguish their work from that of other families. For
example, a basket maker may weave or coil a "signature" into the
basket's design. I received my family signature in an unusual way.
When I moved to South Carolina with my husband and six
children, I knew I had come home to my ancestral lands. My
great-great-great grandmother Margaret Basket made baskets for
her tribe in and around Virginia during the 1800s, but, of course,
I never knew her and didn't receive the family design. My design
was revealed to me, however, in a series of dreams about a bowl-

shaped basket with a black, lightning design. The dreams occurred every night for four nights. Upon waking after the fourth night, I made the basket, and the dreams ceased. A few months later, I felt "called" outside during a thunderstorm. As I closed the door behind me, lightning flashed over my head and struck the door. For me, this experience authenticated the lightning design I had woven. (To this day, my husband is anxious when close to me during thunderstorms!)

I believe, as do other Native Americans, that I am weaving a part of my life into the baskets I create. Although part of my personality is incorporated into the basket, however, the basket also possesses its own spirit. Some baskets I coil are very powerful. Let me share an experience that I feel demonstrates that power. I visited Matilda, a Gullah-Afro friend, at her basket stand on Highway 17 in Mount Pleasant, South Carolina, to show her the Thunder Being basket that was given to me in my dreams. We compared the similar coiling technique we used in our baskets and commented on differences in our basket materials. As she held my basket, I was prompted to say, "Sometimes I feel the power of this basket so strongly that I feel lightning could just jump right in here!" At that instant, from the overcast sky, a lightning bolt flashed over the stand. Experiences like this make me feel that there are no accidents — all things are connected.

MINIATURE BASKETS

In many Native American tribes, miniature baskets are woven to give as gifts that show the skills of the best basket makers. Many times a miniature basket sells for almost the same price as a full-scale basket using the same technique and materials.

The making of miniature baskets is a unique and specialized field, and not everyone has the patience or finger dexterity to make miniature baskets. Not all basket makers can work in the scale of true miniatures, in which 1 inch is equal to 1 foot. I view miniature baskets as sculpture, however, and often produce miniatures as prototypes of baskets I later make full size. In the relatively short amount of time it takes to complete a miniature, I can evaluate my design idea and get a dependable sense of whether or not it will work as a full-scale basket. On pages 90–91 and 94, you will see all the baskets described in the next two chapters (with the exception of the lidded heart basket) in both a full-scale and a miniature version of the same basket. I have included with the directions for each full-scale basket some suggestions for the kind and amount of materials required for you to make your own miniature versions. The technique for miniature basketry is the same as for a full-scale basket. The difference is only in the size of the materials. Experimenting with miniatures allows one to create contemporary expressions of traditional forms using untraditional techniques and materials. Beginning basket makers will find it easier to learn to make a full-scale basket than a miniature. Once you have made a basket or two, however, you may decide to try miniatures.

MAKING YOUR OWN COILED BASKETS

An elder Native American basket maker was once asked if she feared sharing her basketry skills with others who might copy her work and then put her out of a job. She laughed and wisely said, "I like to share what I do with others. As for their copying my style, it will take them the same thirty years it took me to get to the place where I now stand!"

In teaching basketry at conventions in various locations around the country, I have found that most students expect a completed basket of size in six hours or less. It takes time, however, and I must say to them, "Life isn't a destination, it's a journey." I have found that a weekend is usually enough time to share my skills and stories with students, and to enable them to understand and make a variety of coiled baskets.

In this chapter, you are introduced to several procedures involved in coiling baskets. Creating a coiled basket is in some ways similar to creating a piece of pottery. A length of coil material, such as pine needles or cattail leaves, is wound around a center start (see page 59) and sewn to the preceding row. The basket is built and shaped by manipulating the placement of the coil as it is stitched in place. You may work from either the inside or the outside of the basket; I prefer to work from the inside. No matter which way you do it, however, you must constantly check to see that your stitches are correctly placed on the other side.

If you know in advance what to expect, you will find it easier to play with the materials. To make a coiled basket you must first learn the properties of the natural materials you will be using, as well as various common stitching techniques, including how to work in a new piece of raffia (the thread) when the old piece ends. The patterns in this chapter are all variations of the wrapped start used to create the oval shape.

PINE-NEEDLE COILED BASKETS

Pine-needle baskets were popularized by Mrs. M. J. McAfee of West Point, Georgia, who first used pine needles to make her husband a hat during the Civil War, when blockades made hats unavailable. After the war, she taught others, who incorporated different techniques and materials into the traditional pine-needle baskets we see today. As was mentioned earlier, Native

LEGENDS OF THE PINE

To the Iroquois, law and peace are the same — so much so, that the symbol for both law and peace is the Great White Pine. As the tree pierces the sky and reaches toward the sun, it lifts the thoughts of the Iroquois to the meanings of peace. Its branches, on the other hand, signify the shelter, security, and protection found under the shadow of the law. The roots of the tree stretch to the four corners of the earth. They are extensions of the law, and their peace embraces all humankind.

For the Cherokee, the pine originated from the mishap of seven naughty boys. These boys played a stone game too much. Their mothers scolded them. Because the scolding did no good, the mothers served the boys stones for dinner. The disgruntled boys went to the council house to dance. As they danced, they asked to be taken away. They began to rise in the air. Six of the boys became the Pleiades, but the seventh was pulled back to the earth by his mother. He struck the ground so hard that he sank into it. The grieving mother cried over the spot where her son fell. The earth, damp with her tears, sprouted a seedling that grew into the pine. The soul of the seventh brother joined his brothers in the sky, but he is seen only faintly. The pine is thus of the same nature as the stars, full of bright light.

Americans also used pine needles in their baskets; these were usually sewn together with an overcast stitch.

Shortly after moving to South Carolina, I dreamed about chocolate-brown pine needles waving in the wind. After some searching for long-needle pines, I was introduced to a ranger at the Francis Marion Forest Service near Charleston, who showed me how to pick green pine needles without damaging the tree. If you take only needles from the portion of the branch closest to the trunk of the tree, you are removing needles that will fall naturally in the spring and autumn of that year. When I asked the ranger if there was a place in the forest where needles were brown and already fallen, he took me into another part of the forest. Here, loggers had left the tops of long-leaf pine trees lying on the forest floor — waiting for me. It was exactly the place in my dream. All things are connected!

Pine needles make an excellent basketry material when bundled together to form a coil that is then stitched together with a thread, such as raffia. The needles vary in thickness and coarseness. Southern pine needles are long, from 12 to 18 inches, and are preferred by many pine-needle basket makers. These are available from sources listed on page 151.

Because fresh green pine needles shrink as they dry, they must be dried before use, or the stitches that hold the coil will loosen as the needles dry. Dried in the shade, needles will retain a light mint green color. Dried in the sun, southern pine needles become chocolate brown in color; pine needles in other areas of the country dry in a range of colors, from off-white to bluish gray.

If you are able to gather your own dry pine needles, rake them from beneath the tree and sort them so that all the needles point in the same direction. Snip off the sheath ends. Clean them with a little soap and water before you use them.

Dry pine needles can be stored indefinitely. They may become brittle over time, however, and should be soaked before you coil them, or they will break. They must be soaked until they are supple enough to be tied in knots. If you soak them too long, however, they can mold. Hot water makes them pliable more quickly, but don't pour boiling water directly on the needles, or you will remove their natural sheen. Soak only enough needles to begin the base of your basket; the amount required depends on the thickness of the coil you are making.

STITCHING MATERIAL: RAFFIA

Raffia, which is obtained from a type of palm tree, is used to bind the coils together. Raffia has been imported from Madagascar (an island off the southeast coast of Africa) into the United States since the end of the Civil War. Native Americans have used raffia since that time, but before the introduction of raffia, Native Americans in the Southeast used Indian hemp to bind their baskets. Indian hemp, a type of dogbane and a common weed in this area, dries during autumn. After it is gathered, the thin outer bark is removed by rubbing the stems between the palms of the hands. This leaves long, white, fibrous material that must then be corded (two strands of material twisted against each other). Because of the labor involved in this process, most basket makers now use raffia.

Purchase only natural, untreated raffia for basket making. The raffia available in most craft stores is undesirable because it is usually treated with a fire-retardant chemical that turns it a yellowish color; this raffia is waxy to the touch and shreds easily. Untreated raffia can be ordered from various basketry suppliers (see page 151). It comes in a braid, like a "pigtail."

If the raffia strands are too thick for the size coil you are making, they will cover too much of the coil material. To avoid this, split the raffia in half with a needle.

Always thread the thick end of the raffia into your needle first, so that when you stitch, you will be pulling the raffia through *with* the grain of the plant and thus avoid shredding the raffia. I use a #14–18 darning needle for full-scale baskets and a small sewing needle for miniatures.

When your piece of raffia is too short to use (or when it breaks), you will have to begin a new piece. First, end the old piece by placing the threaded needle at the point where the last stitch came through the coil. Slip the needle at an angle through two or more coils, and cut the raffia off an inch from the basket. Next, begin the new piece by threading the needle and placing it at an angle opposite the angle from which you just ended the old piece. Bring the needle through the basket over the last stitch where you ended the raffia, and continue stitching.

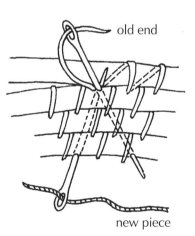

old end

new piece

Starting a new piece of raffia

WHEAT AND FERN STITCHES

The stitches in the baskets that follow are the wheat stitch and the fern stitch. A wheat stitch looks like a V. Successive rows of this stitch form straight vertical paths up the side of the basket. The stitch gets its name from the fact that the paths resemble the head on a shaft of wheat. Place stitches close together — ⅛ inch or less apart. For example, the pine-needle oval basket (page 59) has six wheat stitches along each side of the wrapped start and three stitches at each end of the start. As you place your stitches to the left, turn the basket to the right. For specific instructions, see Steps 3–5, page 60.

The fern stitch is a version of the wheat stitch, with an additional step that turns it into a three-prong stitch (see Steps 10–11, pages 60–61).

USING A GAUGE

In order to create coils of equal diameter, basket makers slide a bundle of coil material through a gauge. This is called *feeding the tail.* For the baskets that follow, a large drinking straw or a ⁵⁄₁₆-inch brass compression sleeve is suitable to use as a gauge. (Brass compression sleeves are available at hardware stores.) If you are right handed, hold the gauge in your left hand, and fill it firmly with core material. Save yourself from being poked unnecessarily by inserting the pine needles pointed ends first into the gauge. The gauge should slide over this core smoothly and firmly. As you wrap and stitch the coil to form the basket, slide the gauge back and add more coil material as needed to make one long, continuous coil of even thickness.

PINE-NEEDLE OVAL BASKET

8½" wide x 10¾" long x 2½" high

You can work on either the inside or outside of the basket, but do choose one or the other and work consistently on that side for the entire project. It is shown in color on page 90.

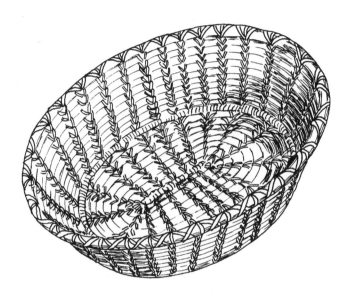

FULL-SCALE BASKET

Pine needles: 5 ounces of 6" (or longer) needles

Natural, untreated raffia: 1–2 ounces

MINIATURE BASKET
(⅝" x ¾" x ¼")

Raffia: one strand, finely split

Pine needles: eight 6" needles (or longer)

1. Soak the needles as described on page 56. Feed the tail, pointed ends in first, until it will support the gauge without slipping (see page 58). Thread the needle with raffia so that you will be pulling the wide end of the raffia through the coil first. With the index finger of the hand that is holding the filled gauge, position ½ inch of the narrow end of the raffia on top of the coil, an inch away from the end. Wrap the raffia once around the coil at that point, leaving 1 inch at the end of the coil unwrapped. (This end will be covered in Step 6.) Wrap the coil for 2 inches, completely covering it and incorporating the narrow end of the raffia as you wrap. This completely wrapped section, called the **start,** is the center of the basket, and its length roughly determines the finished dimensions of the basket. The wrapped start should be the length you want your finished basket *minus* its finished width:

length – width = start

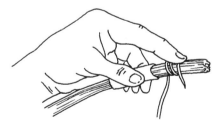

STEP 1

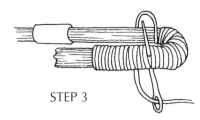

STEP 3

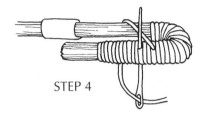

STEP 4

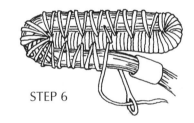

STEP 5

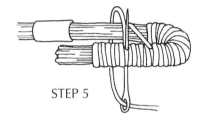

STEP 6

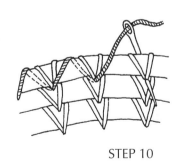

STEP 10

2. Bend the tail back against this wrapped start.

3. The coil is sewn to the wrapped start with the **wheat stitch.** To make the first stitch, take the threaded needle over the unwrapped portion of the coil and come up through the wrapped coil, taking up about one-third of the thickness of the coil. This makes the right side of the first V.

4. Hold the raffia to the right, out of the way of the needle. Again bring the threaded needle over the coil, about ⅛ inch to the left of the first vertical stitch. As in Step 3, bring the needle up through about one-third of the wrapped coil. Pull the raffia through to make the slanted, left-hand side of the V.

5. Bring the needle over the coil again. This time pierce the coil at the same point as in Step 4, to create the vertical part of the next V.

6. Continue stitching in this manner to secure the unwrapped coil to the wrapped one below it. As you near the end of the wrapped coil, take the 1 inch of unwrapped coil end and bend it back on itself and include it in the coil you are stitching. Take several extra fern stitches as you make the turn around the start.

7. When you begin stitching around the second side, make the wheat stitches align with those on the first side. Continue stitching until you have stitched the coil completely around the wrapped center and are back where you began.

8. On the second round, place each wheat stitch so that the V fits into the V in the round below. Examine the back of the base you are coiling. Note that you will have to slant your needle in order to get the V positioned correctly on both back and front.

9. Repeat this pattern for eleven rounds.

10. As the base gets larger, the distance between the stitches on the sides does not change much, but the distance between each stitch on the ends enlarges greatly. If you allow the distance between stitches to become too great, the basket will no longer hold together firmly. For this reason, you must use **fern stitch** to carry the lines of stitching out to the full width of the base. Fern stitch is done in two parts. First, complete an entire round with wheat stitch. Second, stitch the completed round in the *opposite direction*, inserting the needle into the point of each V on the outside of the basket to create a three-prong stitch. Take care that the needle enters and exits at the point of the V on both back and front of the basket.

11. When stitching successive rows, pierce the middle stitch of the fern stitch in the round below to create the first vertical stitch of wheat stitch (as illustrated in Step 15, below). Complete a round in wheat stitch, then reverse direction and again fern stitch the wheat-stitched coil. Complete three rounds of fern stitch. There should now be a total of fourteen coils in the base.

12. For the next round, wrap the coil completely with raffia, catching in about one-third of the coil below at half-inch intervals. This makes a firm foundation on which to build the sides.

SHAPING THE SIDES

13. On the coil completed in Step 12, mark with a piece of colored thread the point even with the beginning of the second round of stitching in the basket base; this is where you will begin to build up the sides. **To flare the sides outward,** place the first coil on top of the coil just completed; set the coil slightly (at about a 45-degree angle) toward the outside. (Note that **to make straight sides,** you would place the coil *directly on top of the coil below.* **To flare the sides inward** you would place the coil to the *inside.*) Use wheat stitch to attach the coils on the sides, following the pattern established on the base *and* making an additional line of stitches between each established line. Let the sides of the basket flare out slightly as you build them up. Complete nine rounds.

14. Set the tenth coil slightly to the outside to make a graceful lip. Attach this round with fern stitch, for a decorative finish.

15. Three stitches before completing the tenth round, taper the end of the coil by cutting it at an acute angle so that it rests flatly and evenly on the top. The join should be barely perceptible.

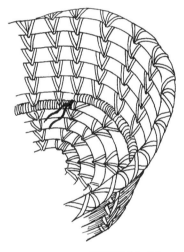

STEPS 13–15

CATTAIL COILED BASKETS

I enjoy using cattails for coiling because they grow to be 9 feet long! This makes it quick to create even large baskets. I used cattails to make fifteen 30" x 72" sleeping mats for the movie remake of *The Last of the Mohicans*, as well as a laundry-basket-style container (30" x 28" x 18") for the new television series "Young Indiana Jones Chronicles." In an episode of the latter, Indy's dog leaps into the basket and floats up into the air, lifted by a patchwork hot-air balloon.

You can create a heart-shaped basket by beginning with a wired, bendable wrapped start or by building it around teneriffes. Because the lacy teneriffes are impractical for a basket bottom, I prefer using them on lids and handles only.

The heart pattern is both traditional and contemporary. Native American designs have incorporated the heart symbol for generations. The Cherokee have a twill pattern called Double Chiefs' Hearts. Only basket makers chosen by the tribe to carry on the tradition and skilled enough to accomplish the design are given the stories behind it. While waiting to learn the traditional tales, I devise my own stories, which reflect my decision to follow my heart even though my path is different from others.

PREPARING MATERIALS

Before frost in your area, cut green cattail leaves after they have grown to their fullest height. Cut individual leaves above the root crown. Do not allow the leaves to remain attached to the thick stalk, as they need good circulation or the material is likely to mold. Stand them on the floor with the thicker ends down in an old-fashioned **stook,** and let them dry thoroughly. Do not stack them on top of each other. Leaves dried in shade will retain a light green color. Use a needle or your fingernail to split the leaves lengthwise into at least four strips before using them in your coil. Especially when you make small baskets, you will need to split very large leaves.

The leaves must be soaked in water before they can be used to begin a basket. If you attempt to use dry materials for the wrapped start, where the turns are sharp and tight, the materials will simply crack and break. Soak them until they are supple enough to be tied into knots — about three hours. Hot water hastens this process. I've found that the bathtub is an excellent soaking place for my larger materials. Time this soaking period around your family routine — some may object to showering with weeds!

Like fresh material, wet material shrinks slightly as it dries. For this reason, wrap your starts tightly, leaving just enough room to get your needle and raffia thread through. After coiling about three rows out from the center, try using dry material in your core. If the dry material does not break as it is bent, you may continue using it for the rest of the basket.

DYEING CATTAIL LEAVES

I dye cattail leaves outdoors in an adapted 55-gallon metal drum. We cut the drum in half lengthwise, removed one end from each half, and welded the two halves together to make a long trough. We set the trough up on a few bricks, and keep a wood fire going underneath to heat the dye bath. I fill this trough three-quarters full of water, to which I add two or three packages of Rit dye. I then bring the dye water to a boil. I place the split, soaked leaves into the boiling dye bath and stir them frequently for several hours until their pithy middles are colored. I remove the dyed cattail leaves from the dye bath with a thick stick, wash and cool them off with the garden hose, and then dip them in a vinegar-and-water (equal parts) solution to set the color. We live in rural South Carolina on 400 acres, but our house faces a busy thoroughfare. My whole dyeing day is spent under the casual glances of hurried travelers who most likely do not understand my ruminations over the hot cauldron!

TENERIFFES

If you wish, you may make a plain lid, just like the base. A very decorative, impressive lid, however, features a triplet of raffia-covered teneriffes. A teneriffe is a wire shape, wrapped on the edges and filled with woven stitchery. Adapted from a European embroidery art, teneriffes give baskets a delicate, lacy touch.

You can use brass rings (available in craft stores) for teneriffes, but the metal is usually thick and disproportionately large next to a 3/16-inch coil. An alternative is to make your own rings out of 16-gauge copper wire. Copper oxidizes slowly and thus does not discolor the raffia. To make the rings, hammer small nails into a wooden board, forming the outline of any shape you wish to create. Scrub the copper wire thoroughly to remove any chemical fluxes, wrap it around the nails, and solder the ends together. This process sounds easier than it is. If not done properly, solder joints tend to weaken and break after a time. Also, conspicuous bulges may show where the ends join. If you don't want to do the soldering yourself, your neighborhood radiator repair shop may be willing to do it for you. You can also purchase teneriffes. Jeannie McFarland (Baskets and Bullets) sells reasonably priced, well-made teneriffes in various sizes and shapes. For her address, see page 151.

CARING FOR ANTIQUE BASKETS

It is important to note that antique coiled basketry, especially baskets with handles, may contain metal. A friend once asked me to repair her antique pine-needle basket. She had been using it to warm buns in her microwave! Not only did the heat make the basket very brittle, but metal can damage microwaves.

HEART-SHAPED CATTAIL BASKET WITH TENERIFFE LID

6" wide x 8½" long x 2" high

This delightful lidded basket (shown on color page 90) is not as difficult to create as you might think.

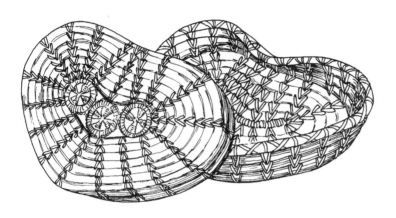

HEART-SHAPED BASE

1. Begin your coil, using the same technique described for a pine-needle coil on page 59. Insert the leaves into the gauge thick end first. Wrap the start with raffia and insert the 4-inch piece of wire into the middle of the gauge, where it won't show. Holding the coil in your left hand, wrap for 4 inches. To get the heart shape, bend the wrapped portion in half to form an open V. As you coil around this V-shaped start, the basket base will develop a heart shape.

2. Using the wheat stitch, as in Steps 3–5, page 60, stitch six rounds circling this heart-shaped center. In a heart-shaped basket, stitches placed above the cleft of the heart come closer together as the base coils progress; you may have to merge two lines of stitching into one. Conversely, lines of stitches on the ends widen very quickly. Plan for this by placing four or five stitches very close together at the ends of the start on the first round.

3. Shape the sides by placing four coils directly on top of each other, except at the cleft of the heart. Sharply flare the coil to the

MATERIALS

Raffia: 1½ to 2 ounces

Copper wire: 4" piece of 16-gauge

Cattails (*Typha* spp.): 8 ounces

Brass rings: three 1" diameter

Gauge: ⅜" brass compression sleeve

Rit dye: two or three packages

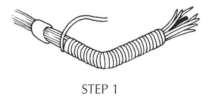

STEP 1

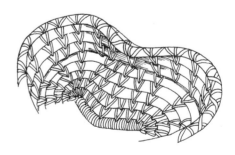

STEP 2

inside of the curve each time you come to this spot.

4. For the fourth and last round, use fern stitch (see Step 10, pages 60–61), for a decorative, sturdy finish. Three stitches before you end the fourth round, taper it by cutting the core material at an acute angle so that the tail rests flatly and evenly on the basket (see Step 15, page 61).

CREATING THE TENERIFFES

5. The wire ring is covered with a double buttonhole stitch — one stitch on the outside of the ring alternates with one on the inside. To begin, split a long piece of raffia in half lengthwise. Cut off as much as necessary of the thinner end so that the entire length is about the same width. Fold this piece of raffia in half crosswise, and thrust the folded end through the ring from below. Bring the two ends of raffia from below around the outside of the ring and through the loop. Pull. Place one strand of raffia on the right; and take the other over the ring on the left. One buttonhole stitch now shows on the outside of the ring.

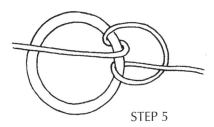

STEP 5

6. To make a stitch on the inside of the ring, bring the left strand of raffia around the outside and up through the center of the ring and the loop it makes. Pull it tight, and slide the knot up so that it rests against the first stitch and forms a stitch inside the ring below the first stitch.

7. The next stitch alternates to the outside. Make a loop in the right strand of raffia close to the ring. Place the loop on top of the ring, below the first two stitches. Bring the end through the ring and through this loop. Pull, to make the second buttonhole on the outside of the ring. Continue in this manner making stitches alternately on the inside and outside of the ring.

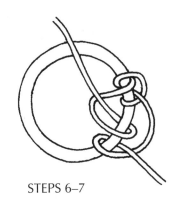

STEPS 6–7

When your pieces of raffia are about 4 inches long, you will have to add another piece of raffia. Prepare as before, and thrust the loop end through the ring where the stitches stop. Make the first stitch, pairing the new strands with the short ends from the first piece. With the paired threads, make two or three stitches on both sides of the ring. To hide the short ends, thread each one through a large-eyed needle, and weave the end through the last three stitches in the same side. Cut it off close to the stitches. Continue in this manner until the entire ring is covered.

8. In this step, you will symmetrically arrange twelve spokes within the prepared ring. Select a thinner piece of raffia, more threadlike than the one used to cover the ring, and thread it into a needle. Starting at the bottom of the ring, secure the raffia to an inside stitch by weaving it back and forth through the stitch next to it a couple of times. Insert the needle into the stitch directly opposite on the ring. Weave to the right in and out of as many stitches as needed to begin the next spoke. (For twelve spokes, divide the circle, by eye, like the face of a clock.) Bring the needle directly across the ring to the opposite side. Continue in this manner until the ring has twelve spokes. When you create the last spoke, weave the raffia to the beginning of the first spoke you made, and follow it to the center of the ring. During the rest of the weaving, treat these two spokes as one. Weave over-one and under-one around all the spokes in the center to secure them at the center hub. You are now ready to weave a pattern.

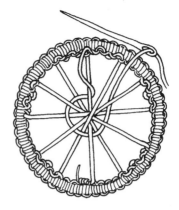

STEP 8

9. Select a group of three spokes to work with first. Weaving over-one, under-one, weave back and forth among the three spokes. Pack the stitching tightly. Weave until you are almost to the ring, but leave a space between your weaving and the inside stitches on the ring. Return to the center of the spokes by carefully inserting the needle on the outside edge of your weaving and sliding it through the weaving to the center of the spokes. The carrying thread must not show on either side of the stitching. Move to the next set of spokes and repeat this procedure. If you need to add raffia, do so at the beginning of a group of three, first taking the thread back through a completed segment and clipping it off at the center. Begin another piece by taking another thin piece of raffia down through a completed segment. Repeat until all sets of spokes are woven. Make three teneriffe rings for this basket.

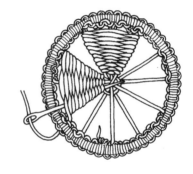

STEP 9

ATTACHING THE TENERIFFES

10. Attach the covered rings by stitching together three or four buttonhole stitches on the outside of abutting rings. Sew them together so that they accurately match the angle of the wrapped beginning in the base of the basket.

11. Fill the gauge with cattail leaves, as for the basket base.

Attach the threaded raffia to the top of the righthand ring by weaving in and out of two or three buttonhole stitches on the outside of the ring. Holding the filled gauge in your left hand, place it against the completed teneriffe. Leave an inch of coil unattached and work counterclockwise. Bring the needle over the fiber coil, behind it and through the buttonhole stitch toward yourself, to make the first stitch of the wheat stitch, as before.

12. Stitch the coil to the three teneriffes until about three stitches before you reach the place you began. Taper-cut the unwrapped beginning of the coil at an acute angle so that it rests flatly and evenly on the edge of the teneriffe.

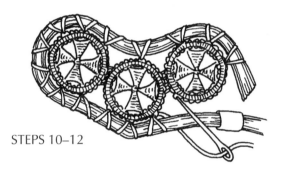

STEPS 10–12

13. Continue to coil around this beginning. After you complete the third round, as you approach the bottom of the heart, bend the coil sharply so that the heart's point becomes more defined.

14. Continue coiling until you have completed seven rounds, or until the lid covers the base. Periodically, as you coil the lid, match it against the completed base to be sure that the size and shape are identical.

15. To begin the sides, place the eighth round at a right angle to the last coil on the lid. Coil three more rounds for the sides. Use fern stitch for the last round.

16. Taper the end of the coil, so that it lies flat.

COILING WITH BULRUSHES

Many types of bulrush exist in numerous locations throughout the United States. (If you order rush from basketry suppliers, do not expect the "real" thing; catalogs generally carry a paper product.)

I have found Midwestern rush to be pithier and softer than the rush growing here in South Carolina; and the Midwestern rush dries a soft green color, whereas South Carolina rush, aged outdoors, turns a beautiful brown. Bulrush should be gathered only every other year in any one area, in order for the stand to flourish. To Native Americans, the best plants are the grandfathers of the species. As such, they are treated with respect and allowed to stay in the field to replenish the supply for basket makers in future generations.

Cut bulrush close to the ground, and follow the same procedure as for drying cattail leaves (see page 62).

MATERIALS

FULL-SCALE BASKET

Raffia: 3 ounces

Bulrush (*Scirpus* spp.):
1 pound of 6–8 feet tall rush

Copper wire: one 8" and
one 24" length of 16-gauge
wire

MINIATURE BASKET
(1¼" x 1½" x ⅞")

Raffia: one finely split
strand

Pine needles: 16

Fine floral wire: one ⅝" and
one 2" length

BULRUSH EGG BASKET

7¾" wide x 10¼" long x 6" high

Some time ago, a miniature collector who participated in a class I taught at the Chicago Botanical Garden added one of these tiny egg baskets to her collection. The curator of the Garden called me after I arrived back home in Jonesville to tell me the following story: The lady who purchased this basket carefully arranged her treasure in her miniature room, which was located near her garage. When the basket was gone the next morning, she theorized that "two bad mice" (as in Beatrix Potter's story, The Tale of Two Bad Mice) had stolen the basket during the night. Other times when she had missed one of her tiny treasures, she had found all or part of the stolen articles in her garage; this time, however, her search brought to light the parts of two missing chairs, but no basket. We all assume that the two mice are happily using their newly pilfered piece. The miniature is shown on color page 94; the full-size version is on page 91.

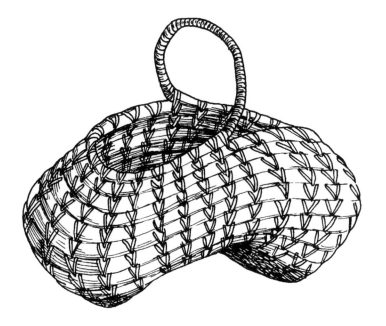

1. Fill a brass compression sleeve with bulrush (see pages 58–59). The ring should be firm on the rush, but not so tight as to shred it. Insert the shorter piece of wire into the center of the rush as in Step 1, page 65.

2. Wrap the start for 6 inches.

3. To create the distinctive shape of the egg basket base, bend the wrapped portion in a V shape. The point of the V will be up in the finished basket, and each end will become one "cheek" of the basket.

4. Use the wheat stitch to attach the coil. (See Steps 3–5, page 60). Four or five stitches must be placed close together at the ends of the start as you wrap the tail around for the first round. Evenly space the other stitches on each side of the coil.

5. Continue to stitch until you have five rounds circling the start.

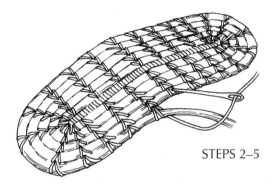

STEPS 2–5

6. At the point aligned with where the basket was started, begin to flare the coils outward and upward for six rounds. (See Step 13, page 61).

7. Coil the basket to the top edge by gradually tapering the coils inward for another seven rounds.

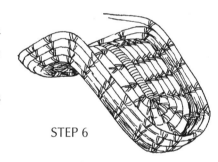

STEP 6

MAKING THE HANDLE

8. To create the handle, at the stitch before you end the last round of coiling, insert the longer piece of wire into the top coil and incorporate it into the unwrapped bulrush in the gauge. Make sure to hide it in the middle, where the wire doesn't show. Take several stitches at this point, to secure the handle to the basket.

9. Completely wrap the rush coil and wire with raffia so that neither shows. When you come to the end of a piece of raffia, bring the threaded needle back through the wrapped coil to secure and end it. Thread the needle with another piece, bring the needle through the wrapped coil, and catch the tail of the raffia under the next few wraps around the coil. Continue wrapping for 8 inches.

Bend the handle over the basket. Place it on the opposite side of the basket, facing in the opposite direction of the handle beginning. Secure it with several stitches.

About 2 inches from the point of attachment, cut the coil at an angle, and using a wheat stitch, stitch it to the top coil. Be sure the wheat stitches align with the rows already in place. Make a couple of small stitches in one place to secure the end, weave the raffia back through the coil, and clip it close to the basket.

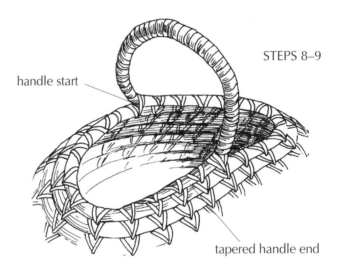

STEPS 8–9

handle start

tapered handle end

TIP FOR MINIATURE BASKET

To make it easier to work with, twist the rush as you sew or braid three thin strips of bulrush together in a continuous braid about 2 yards long. Coil as usual.

BASKETS FOR THE GARDEN

NANCY BASKET

When I first began making pine-needle baskets, I thought mine had to be like everyone else's. I once even scoffed at an Alabama Coushatti woman's pine-needle basket that had absolutely "huge" ⅝-inch coils! (As everyone knows, the "correct" gauge for pine-needle basketry is that of the ³⁄₁₆-inch gauge.) I laughed at the contemporary style of other basket makers, especially the ones living in California. Then Grandfather (God) arranged for me to live in California for a year and a half. My ideas and opinions about basketry and life in general changed rapidly as I sat at the beach and wove a basket from seaweed! My life A.C. (After California) has been truly liberating. When I couldn't find pine needles for months at a time, I made a large-scale laundry basket from the cattail leaves that grew all around us. We had an oval piece of glass cut for the top and used it for a coffee table. Once you've seen the light, you too can create even more exotic and unusual basketry forms. Although your first baskets may not be perfect, neither were mine. It is only after I've made a great many baskets of a very similar nature that "perfection" presents itself. Your basket is not imperfect, it's just asymmetrical! It's okay to be different, as the story of how Grandfather created the snake demonstrates.

GRANDFATHER CREATES SNAKE

Long time ago, when the world was new, Grandfather decided to form a creature from the last bit of clay in his pot. He shaped and molded the clay, and Snake was born.

Grandfather gave Snake eyes to see. The long, thin animal was filled with wonder. Grandfather told Snake to wait, because he needed to go to the river for more clay.

Snake waited a long time, but Grandfather did not return. Snake looked up and saw the stars. He looked down and saw the colors of the earth. The colors intrigued him, so he crawled out of Creation to see what they were. He forgot to wait for Grandfather.

When Grandfather came back, he said, "Where is Snake? I have more clay to finish him." He looked around, saw that Snake had left Creation, and said, "Where is Snake going? He has no legs to walk! How will Snake stay warm with no skin? I wish him well, but I wish he would have waited."

Snake found that he had to crawl on his belly to move around — he didn't know he should have legs. The cold made him shiver and shake — he did not know he was supposed to have skin. He did know that he must get warm or die. Snake saw a bright light on the ground. Could that brightness keep him warm? He crawled toward the light and into a woman's round house, where he began to get warm. When the woman saw him, she screamed and called him ugly! Snake quickly crawled out of the round house and into the cold. Trying to keep warm, he crawled under a rock. From his lonely vantage point, Snake saw another spot of brilliance. Trying once more, he crawled toward the light into a man's round house. The man saw the new thing, took a stick, and beat him! Snake, bruised and battered, left the round house to die. He did not understand why he was so mistreated. He was just different.

Lonely Snake cried. His tears froze his eyes open. To this day, all snakes after him cannot close their eyes. His tail froze and cracked into little pieces. To this day, all rattlesnakes are known by their tails. Carelessly strewn on the ground outside the round house were some beads for a new belt that the man was making. Snake crawled into the beautifully colored beads. Wiggling in the color, he hoped to stay warm. The beads clung to his sticky clay body and a pattern formed on his back. To this day, many snakes have beautiful designs on the skins they beaded for themselves. They still, however, seek places to keep warm.

Different doesn't have to be ugly or bad. Different is just different.

COILING WITH BROOM-SEDGE

Most coiled basketry designs can be made with many different kinds of basketry materials. Accustomed to adapting to change, the People (as most Native American tribes refer to themselves) use the materials growing around them to create their baskets. The Cherokee have treaties with some states to obtain the rare river cane they use in their basketry. Historically, Southwestern basket makers used mostly yucca, but now those who are elderly, as well as those who have moved away from a ready source, purchase horsehair and coil it in the same manner as they would yucca. Some of these basket makers create diminutive horsehair objects that embody human figures and sell for thousands of dollars.

An excellent and economical material that is very appropriate for making rectangular baskets is broom-sedge (*Andropogon virginicus*). This clump-forming plant grows in many parts of the United States. If broom-sedge is unavailable in your area, adapt and use what you have. One possibility is sour dock (*Rumex acetosa*), a dark chocolate-colored weed, which many farm children pick and chew for its sour flavor (hence, its name). Sour dock grows in many areas of the United States. Baskets using this material are more ornamental than functional, however, as the seeds from the plant shed. (See the large basket on page 90.)

An old prairie grass, broom-sedge gets its name because Southerners gathered it to make brooms to sweep their floors. A related species, little bluestem (*Andropogon scoparium*), is a grayish-blue color when it is young. After it matures in the fall, it keeps its long, slender leaves throughout the winter and turns a soft tan. An entire population of this grass grows in the field opposite my 150-year-old studio cabin. Primitive and textural, broom-sedge baskets are Adirondack in feeling. Worked into the basket, the leaves have a hairy look. In one public school where I taught basketry, I found that my more symmetrical students preferred to cut the leaves off, for a more refined, "shaved" look.

Cut dry broom-sedge close to the ground, after the seeds fall to the earth in late autumn. I once cut the plant earlier, before the seeds fell, because I hoped to keep the reddish color. The seeds opened in the classroom, however, and by the end of the week when our baskets were done, we had fluffy seeds 1-inch deep all over the room. Bundle the grass, and store it in a dry place.

BROOM-SEDGE HERB TRAY

7½" wide x 11¼" long x 3" high

This pattern shows how to create a coiled rectangular shape and introduces a fancy four-part handle. This basket is shown on color page 90.

This basket is shown on color page 90.

MATERIALS

FULL-SCALE BASKET

Raffia: 1½ to 2 ounces

Copper wire: two 3' pieces of 16-gauge wire

Broom-sedge *(Andropogon virginicus)* or other field grass: ½ pound

½" brass compression sleeves: two, for gauges

MINIATURE BASKET
(⅞" x 1⅜" x ¼")

Raffia: one strand, finely split

Broom-sedge: two or three thin stalks

Fine floral wire: 2"

BASE AND SIDES

1. Wrap the start for 4½ inches, and bend the tail back against the wrapped start. (See Steps 1–2, pages 59–60.)

2. Begin attaching the coil with wheat stitch, and bend the tail back against the wrapped start. (See Steps 3–5, page 60.) You will need about nine stitches along each side of the start and about five, placed close together, at each end of the start.

3. After the second round, bend two corners sharply at each end of the start to form a rectangle. Pull the stitches tight, so that the base of the basket remains firm.

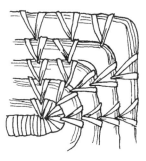

STEP 3

4. Continue building the base in this manner, until you have eight rounds in all.

5. Shape the sides by placing the coils directly on top of each other for five rounds. Make sure to square the corners evenly.

HANDLE

6. When you reach the point above where you began building the sides, insert a piece of wire through the gauge into the middle of the coil material. Push the wire into the coil for 2 or 3 inches. Wrap the tail, allowing the coil material to show through the wrapping, for the next 18 inches to form the first part of the four-piece handle. Bend the wrapped coil where it is attached to the basket and again 14 inches away from this point. With a clothespin, fasten the remaining 4 inches of wrapped core to the top coil on the opposite side of the basket, facing it back toward the same end of the basket from which the coil springs. (Do not cut the coil.)

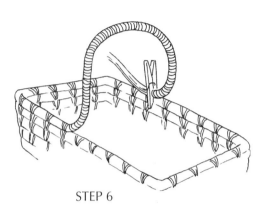

STEP 6

7. To create the second part of the handle, start a new coil by filling a gauge with core material, and insert the other piece of wire into the center of the coil as in Step 6. Leaving the first inch unwrapped, wrap the next 18 inches of this coil. (Do not cut this coil.)

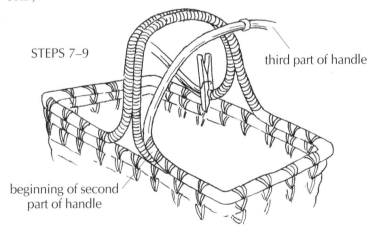

STEPS 7–9

third part of handle

beginning of second part of handle

8. With a clothespin, fasten the 1-inch, unwrapped end of this coil next to where the handle in Step 6 begins. Sew it in place with three wheat stitches.

9. Attach the two handle parts by sewing them together. Use a

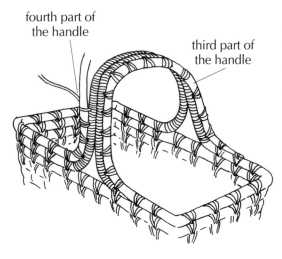

fourth part of the handle

third part of the handle

STEPS 10–11

simple overhand stitch, taking the needle through the middle of the coil. As you sew, shape the second handle part to conform to the first. When you reach the opposite side of the basket, place the second handle part on the top coil, facing back toward the end from which it springs. Using wheat stitch, stitch the coil completely around that end of the basket. When you reach the wrapped handle, use wheat stitch to stitch the coil to the outside of it along its entire length, to form the third part of the handle.

10. When you reach the other side of the basket, cut and taper the end of the handle coil so that it extends three stitches beyond the wrapped handle. Stitch the end to the top coil.

11. Use the remaining tail from the first part of the handle to complete the fourth part of the handle, by stitching it around the end of the basket to the handle and up the side of the handle. Taper the end and stitch it to the top coil, three stitches beyond the handle.

COILING WITH RYE STRAW

Rye straw is not grown in many areas of the U.S., so you may have to use a substitute, such as wheat straw or cattail leaves. One summer, we gathered 5- to 6-foot-tall rye straw, which was grown under high-tension wires; the power company had used the fast-growing rye instead of more costly landscape material. Contact your County Extension Service and ask whether they know of any rye crops in your area that are grown for a similar purpose.

When the green disappears from the stalk, cut the rye straw close to the ground and remove the seed heads. These contain moisture and must be removed from the stalk, or they will mold and turn dark. You can bundle the cut heads together and use them in ornamental dried arrangements. Bundle the armfuls of stalks loosely, and stand them in stooks. When you are ready to use the straw, remove the thin, dull sheath that covers the stalk to reveal the shining golden stalk underneath.

Soak the rye straw for an hour or so in the tub, and then allow it to mellow, wrapped up in a towel.

RYE-STRAW BEE SKEP
8¼" diameter x 7" high

*The bee skep is an example of an outside basket — that is, the
outside is the only part you see. Skep is the Old English word for
basket. Bee skeps were used as beehives until the middle 1800s,
when they were prohibited because they could not be properly
cleaned. The possible contamination of honey was more easily
controlled by using the now-familiar square, white wooden boxes.
Bee skeps still make attractive ornaments in the garden, however.
This pattern introduces a knot start, needed to create round baskets.
To Native Americans, the shape of harmony created the circle, and
thus the circle represents life, unity, and equality — perfection.
When a round basket springs to life in my hands, I am reminded
that we all stand in different areas of the circle — together.
This basket is shown on color page 91.*

MATERIALS

FULL-SCALE BASKET

Rye straw (*Secale* spp.):
½-pound, 5'-6' or longer

Raffia: 1-2 ounces natural,
untreated

⅝-inch brass compression
sleeve, for a gauge

Copper wire: 18" 16-gauge

MINIATURE BASKET
(¾" x 1⅛")

Rye straw: one 5' stalk,
sectioned into quarters

Raffia: one strand, finely
split

Fine floral wire: ½"

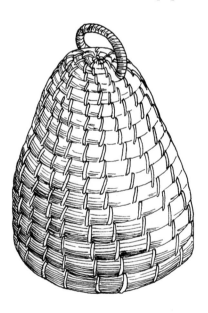

1. You will begin the skep at the top and work toward the base.
Bee skeps are open at the bottom, like an upside-down bowl. Tie
a knot in the blunt end of a group of seven damp rye stalks, leaving
a half inch of fibers at the end. Pull the knot tightly. (Or, you can
just bend the stalks over on themselves.) Incorporate the short
ends of the knot into the tail, and treat the two as a unit. Slip a
⅝-inch gauge over the coil.

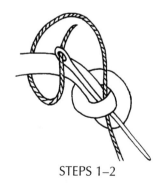

STEPS 1–2

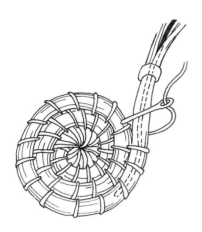

STEPS 3–4

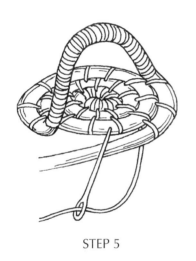

STEP 5

2. Coming from the back to the front, pierce the center of the knot with a needle threaded with raffia. Bring the needle through the knot, leaving a ½-inch end of raffia on the other side. Bring the needle over the coil and back through the knot.

3. Bend the long tail to the left of the knot, so that you will be working counterclockwise. Using an overcast stitch, attach the coil by bringing the raffia over the coil, and piercing the knot with the needle from the outside to the inside, ½ inch to the left of the previous stitch. Repeat this stitch, adding a few lengths of core material to the center of the tail as the tail narrows. Place a gauge on the core material, and gradually add more core material until the gauge fits snugly. Coil out for three rounds.

4. Insert the length of wire into the core material. Wrap a handle for 5 inches, as described in Step 9, pages 71–72.

5. Bring the wrapped handle over the top of the bee skep, and secure it to the coil on the opposite side by taking several stitches in one place.

6. Continue coiling in a counterclockwise direction for one more round. Put each stitch just to the right of the stitch in the previous round to create a swirling pattern. Be sure to place the stitches in the first few rounds close together, as the distance between stitches continues to widen as the basket flares out.

7. After the fourth round, place the tail to the outside edge of the coil below, so that the skep flares out slightly for four rounds.

8. For the next ten rounds, continue the flare, but make it more gradual. Be sure to complete one entire round before you change the slope, or your skep will be asymmetrical.

9. Cut the ends of the rye straw at a rather steep angle so that they rest flatly and evenly on the top coil.

DESIGN ALTERNATIVE

If you want to make a larger bee skep (one that is more to historical and functional scale), increase the coil size to 1 inch in diameter. The amount of rye straw needed to build a basket this size increases by a factor of four.

COILING WITH BRAIDED CORNHUSKS

Cornhusks have been used by Native American tribes for centuries for a wide variety of forms, including tied sleeping mats, twined overshoes, and braided cornhusk masks. I find them to be a very adaptable material for basketry.

We save the cornhusks from all the corn our family of eight eats yearly. We separate the green husks from the cob and dry each one individually. Dried in the shade, they retain a bit of green color; dried in light, shucks from "eatin' corn" dry an off-white color. The shucks sold for tamale making are a bleached white. Husks from Indian corn range from beautiful shades of purple to deep red, and feed-corn shucks dry a harvest-yellow color. The miniature basket shown on page 94 was made with Indian corn-husks that we grew.

To use dried cornhusks, dip them into water for five minutes, and then wrap them in a towel and let them mellow for five minutes more.

Cornhusks are about 9 inches long. To braid, use three husks, secured at the top with a bit of raffia. Attach the tied end to the back of a chair or other secure point with a clothespin, so that you can gently pull on them when you braid. Bring the left strand over the center strand, and pull the middle strand to the left. Bring the right strand over the middle strand, and pull the middle strand to the right. Repeat this procedure. It is very important to stagger the lengths of your cornhusks so that you don't have to add three husks at the same time. Always add new shucks to the middle strand, leaving at least ½ inch sticking out of the braid. This lends strength to the braid. After you sew the braid together, you can snip off the extra ends. Do *not* cut them when the braid is wet, or it will unravel.

For the pattern that follows, I use whole cornhusks to make a thick braid about 1 inch in diameter. To create thinner braids, split the cornhusks before braiding them. I like the bulky, primitive look of this basket, and, of course, because the coiling material is thick, the project is quickly made.

MATERIALS

FULL-SCALE BASKET

Cornhusks *(Zea mays)*: 8 ounces

Raffia: 1–2 ounces natural, untreated

Copper floral wire: 12"

MINIATURE BASKET
(1⅝" x 2½" x ½")

Cornhusk: 1, finely split

Raffia: 1 strand, finely split

BRAIDED-CORNHUSK FLOWER-GATHERING BASKET
9" wide x 13¼" long x 3½" high

This pattern evolved from an experience I had with an object I created from 26 yards of braided cattails. The shape of the basket I made reminded me of a sunflower. Not everyone shared my vision, however. When I submitted it to a show, competition judges thought it looked like a wastepaper basket! They said it was too tall for the materials and techniques used. Since not all judges appreciate all types of basketry, I rather high-handedly dismissed their comments. When an anonymous admirer stopped to tell me how much she liked my wastepaper basket, I reconsidered the validity of the judges' opinions! Because the rebelliousness in my contemporary soul prevails, I will continue to use traditional materials to create nontraditional shapes. I realize, however, that many people have preconceived ideas about the shapes of certain baskets. I have found when I stay within the boundaries of classical pottery forms and traditional shapes — such as that of this gathering basket (shown on color page 91) — I don't err.

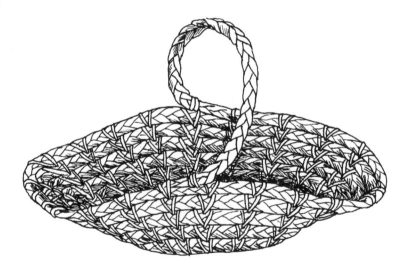

1. Braid cornhusks to make a 12–15 yard braid.

2. Bend 4 inches of braid back against the length of braid. Starting at the bend, stitch the two parts together using wheat

stitch (see page 60). Place the stitches about ½ inch apart, and keep the braid flat. Fold the braid around the end and stitch this section along the other side of the 4-inch start. You will need about five stitches along each side of the start, and five stitches, close together, at each end.

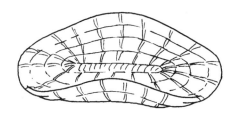

STEP 2

3. Continue stitching for four rounds to create the base of the basket. Keep the braid flat throughout.

4. To create the distinctive shape — flat on the ends and curved up at the handle — keep the braid flat at the ends of the oval only, and bend the braid up as you stitch it to the round below on the sides of the basket. Complete four more rounds in this manner.

STEP 3

5. One stitch before you complete the fourth round and begin the handle, unravel 2 inches of the braided cornhusk. Lay the end of the wire on the center strand. Roll the husk over the wire, so that the wire doesn't show, and re-braid, incorporating the wire, until the handle is the desired length. I constantly check the length by putting it in position and relying on my eye to tell me when it is right for the size and shape of the basket.

6. Secure the braided handle to the basket by taking several stitches in one place. Bend the handle over the basket, and turn it toward the other end, as shown on page 82. This adds a gentle twist to the handle. Secure the handle on the other side with several stitches. Clip off the wire so it doesn't show. Cut the end of the braid at an acute angle so that it rests flatly and evenly on the top coil. Make two or three stitches on the side of the basket to anchor the handle firmly.

STEP 5

DESIGN ALTERNATIVES

You can create contemporary-looking, designer flower baskets with dyed cornhusks. To dye husks, wet them and gently simmer them in a Rit dye bath for ½ hour or until they are the color you want. (Be sure to use the pan only as a dye pot once it has been used for this purpose.) Rinse the dyed husks in a half-vinegar, half-water solution to set the dye.

❦ PORTFOLIO OF BASKETS ❦

The color pages that follow contain photographs of natural baskets created by the contributors to this book. For complete instructions on how to make the baskets included as projects, see the map key on page 86. The baskets that are not keyed to projects illustrate more complicated designs that the basket artists hope will inspire you to explore new ideas, once you have mastered the simpler techniques they describe in detail.

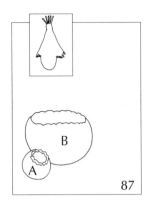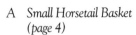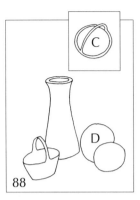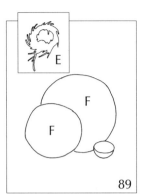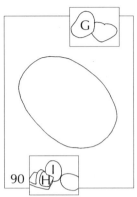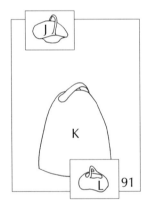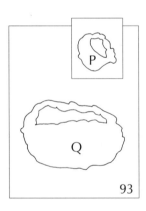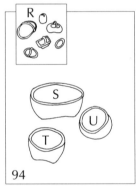

A Small Horsetail Basket (page 4)

B Openwork Basket (page 7)

C Wild Willow-Ware (page 31)

D Openwork Willow Bowl (page 22)

E Red-Osier Dogwood Wreath (page 50)

F Round Red-Osier Dogwood Basket (page 45)

G Heart-Shaped Cattail Basket with Teneriffe Lid (page 65)

H Broom-Sedge Herb Tray (page 76)

I Pine-Needle Oval Basket (page 59)

J Braided-Cornhusk Flower-Gathering Basket (page 82)

K Rye-Straw Bee Skep (page 79)

L Bulrush Egg Basket (page 70)

M Diagonal-Plaited Birch-Bark Pouch (page 101)

N Kittenhead Birch-Bark Basket (page 109)

O Miniature Plaited Birch-Bark Laundry Basket (page 105)

P Vine-Gathering Basket with Rib Construction (page 129)

Q Random-Weave Market Basket of Honeysuckle Vine (page 125)

R Miniatures of Nancy Basket's full-size baskets (pages 51-83)

S Spoon Basket (page 141)

T Shaker Horsehair Basket (page 145)

U Coiled Horsehair Basket (page 148)

❧ *Equisetum baskets by Diana Macomber*

୬ *Willow baskets by Sandy Whalen*

🍂 *Red-Osier Baskets and Wreath by Maryanne Gillooly*

PHOTOS (THIS PAGE) BY CAROL J. JESSOP

Coiled Baskets by Nancy Basket

🐦 *Coiled Baskets by Nancy Basket*

🌰 *Bark Baskets by Cass Schorsch*

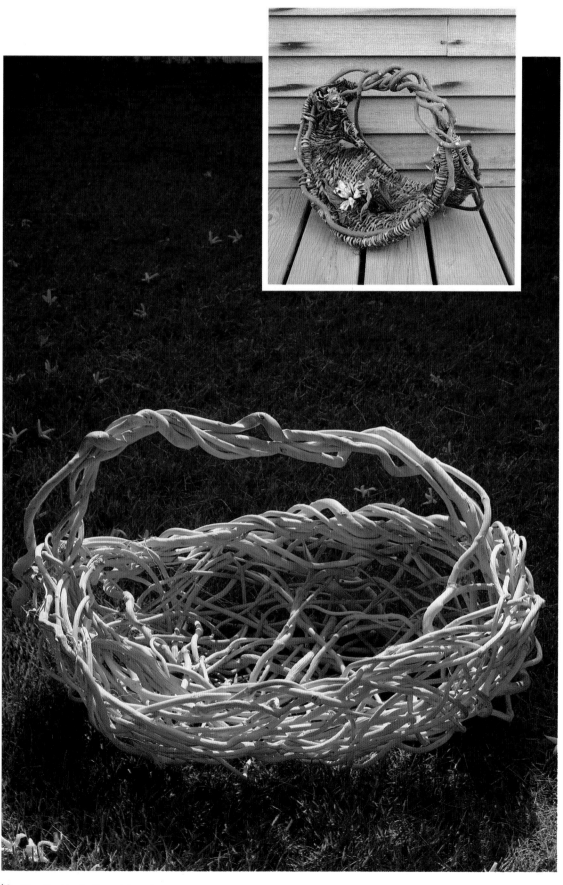

Vine Baskets by Doris Messick

❧ *Miniature Baskets by Nancy Basket (top), Horsehair Baskets by Gerrie Kennedy (bottom)*

BARK BASKETRY
CASS SCHORSCH

If you have not tried working with barks, maybe this chapter will entice you to give it a try. Not many people work with tree barks, so you will have to find your way around this area of basketry somewhat on your own. Because I had to teach myself what I know about birch-bark preparation, I have found bark basketry techniques most challenging. The rewards, however, have been most gratifying. This form of basketry has sharpened my senses and made me more aware of my surroundings. Bark-gathering time is in the spring of the year — a time of reawakening and rebirth, and a wonderful time to be in the woods. The smells and colors stimulate all of one's senses. As well as being pleasing and fascinating to the eye, each bark has its own distinctive smell and feels like leather to the touch. The sound of the bark coming off the logs quickens the sense of hearing, causing one to be more aware of other sounds in the woods.

I would like to invite you to share some history, some information about harvesting and preparing materials, and some projects to get you on your way in an exciting new area of basketry.

The birch tree (*Betula papyrifera*) grows abundantly in the Northern Hemisphere; there are approximately fifteen species of birch native to this part of the world. The Birch Family (*Betulaceae*) includes alders (*Alnus*), hornbeams (*Carpinus*), and hop hornbeams (*Ostrya*).

A deciduous tree, the birch is fast growing (it reaches a height of 40 to 60 feet) but short lived (it matures at 60 to 80 years). Each tree usually bears both the male seed, in the form of a long catkin, and the female, in a conelike cluster.

The wood of paper birch (also called white birch and canoe birch) is used for items such as toothpicks, clothespins, spools, broom handles, ice-cream sticks, and pulpwood. The outstanding feature of the white birch tree is its everlasting outer bark. It is important to note that I say *outer bark*. In most bark basketry, it is the inner bark or cambium layer that is used. In birch bark basketry, however, it is always the outer bark.

As far back as history takes us, people living in the northern latitudes (what is now Siberia, Finland, Sweden, Alaska, and northern North America) have depended on the birch tree. From prehistoric times until only a hundred years ago, most shelters in these areas used birch bark as a roofing material, because of its waterproof qualities.

In Alaska, folded and stitched pieces of birch bark were used as cooking utensils. In some cases, hot stones were dropped into the bark containers in order to heat the contents, but it is also said that these containers could be put directly on the fire, so long as the container was kept full of food. These Alaskan natives commonly used hundreds of folded containers for gathering sap from the maple trees in spring. **Mukuks,** as they called these very strong, long-lasting containers, were folded with the sap side out, which made them more durable. Bark harvested during the winter or early spring retained a thin layer of inner bark. After the piece was folded and stitched together with lengths of spruce root, a design, such as a deer, beaver, fish, or flower, could be scratched into this layer of inner bark.

The most widely known way in which birch was used in North America is for the canoe. Native American boats were made of large pieces of bark stitched together with the roots of the spruce and stretched over a frame of white cedar. The stitched seams were then sealed with balsam pitch. For its first builders, this light, durable, waterproof craft must have revolutionized transportation — a floating horse, you might say.

In Finland, Siberia, and Sweden, birch bark was used for roofing and storage containers and travel gear, as well as for scoops and other cooking implements. The Laplanders, being nomadic people, also gathered large quantities of bark with which to barter, as well as to use for storage and for travel equipment. All of these countries are noted for their bark containers, with tops and bottoms made of wood, and sides made of pieces of bark dovetailed together. The sides consisted of two layers of bark, with intricate designs cut in the top layer to expose the layer beneath. If the bark was collected in winter or early spring, designs were also etched into the soft layer of inner bark.

The Swedish are known for their diagonal birch bark weaving. Backpacks, arrow quivers, knife sheaths, place mats, and the "one-mile" shoe are just a few of the items made with birch bark. Because the Swedish remove the bark from the tree diagonally, they have extremely long pieces for their weaving. These diagonally woven containers are flexible, and thus not as strong and stable as the folded pieces made by Native Americans.

After such a long, successful history, it may be surprising that some, myself included, are just discovering the wonderful possibilities of birch bark. I started weaving baskets seven years ago. For the first few years, I took classes to learn different styles and techniques, but I always used preprocessed, rattan materials. Living in the woods of northern Michigan, I wanted to utilize the natural materials that were native to North America, and especially the area in which I lived. After we had been on a walk in the woods, my friend Tom McColley suggested I try working with birch bark, as it is so prolific in our area. That same fall, our neighbors cut down two very large birch trees, and I asked if I could take the bark off the logs. No problem — they didn't want to take the chance of bringing insects into their house when they brought in the firewood. That opportunity was a beginning that has led to some of my most rewarding baskets. There is something mystical, comforting, and so totally satisfying about creating a basket from materials you have gathered and prepared yourself.

When people ask where I get the patterns for my miniature baskets, I reply that some are simply taken from my favorite full-size baskets. As no two trees are the same size, some of my miniatures are larger in scale than others. When you create your own, you will have to approximate each time — there are no absolutes.

HARVESTING BIRCH BARK

The best time to harvest any tree for its bark is when the sap is up, which is in late spring and early summer. I feel the best time to harvest birch is June. Bark harvested earlier is "winter bark," which is what you want for folded or dovetail containers; it is also the bark to use if you want to scratch designs into it.

If you want to cut any trees, or even remove bark from fallen trees, first and foremost, obtain permission from the landowner. This includes national- and state-owned land. Get in touch with your local Department of Natural Resources office, and tell them what you want to do. You will be surprised how helpful they are. You won't need much — one mature birch tree will supply one individual with enough bark to keep busy weaving for months.

Look for a straight tree, 8 inches or larger in diameter, with as few knots as possible. An 8-inch-diameter tree will give you weaving strips approximately 16 inches long. The larger the tree, the longer the strips. Although most barks are cut on the vertical for spokes and weavers, birch bark is cut on the horizontal, parallel to the lenticel lines (the breathing pores). You will make a vertical cut to remove the bark, but the weaving material will be cut on the horizontal of the bark.

Since birch trees often grow in the moist soils of swamps and river borders and have shallow root systems, it is often possible to find trees that have blown over during the winter. These trees are a wonderful source for bark. I stay away from trees that have fungus growing on them. Such a specimen is likely to have been worked over by woodpeckers before it fell and will be riddled with little holes. I prefer to cut a tree down rather than take bark from a standing tree. Although the debarked section will heal so long as you don't girdle the tree, it will turn gray and become crusty, disfiguring the tree forever.

When you cut a tree down, be sure to check the trees around it. Plan your fall, so that when the tree goes, it will not be scarred by scraping against standing trees. After I fell a tree, I cut it into woodstove-size pieces. I then run my knife down the length of the log, get my fingers under the bark, and peel it off the log.

The size of the tree has nothing to do with the thickness of its bark. I find that trees farther north have thicker bark. Like cedars and black ash, this is a tree that loves long, cold winters.

You will note that bark from fresh fallen trees tends to curl opposite the direction it grew after it is removed from the logs. If allowed to remain curled, in a short time it will be useless for basketry. The most important step after you peel the bark is to flatten it. For this, I use a press made of ¾-inch plywood measuring about 24" x 36" as a base, and a top made of three strips of 1 x 4s attached to the plywood with 6-inch bolts. These strips allow for circulation. When you lay your bark in the press, place it sap side (brown side) to sap side, and white side to white side.

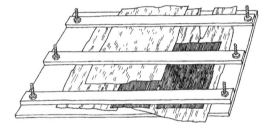

Bark press

This forces the pieces against each other and helps the flattening process. I keep my press outside under a shelter that protects it from rain and snow. If you take the bark into the house, the heat will eventually rob it of all its moisture, making it brittle and useless. I have kept bark outside in a press for two years where it is exposed to natural humidity, and I find it still workable. Always store the press under shelter, and never leave it in the sun, which removes the moisture the same as indoor heat.

Although it is possible to weave with your bark immediately following harvest, the nature of the material is to curl and it is thus best to place it in the press for a month before weaving. Even after being pressed for a month, it sometimes tries to curl. I have found that the pieces closest to the base of the trunk are more apt to lie flat immediately following harvest.

Bark from fallen trees may be moldy on the sap side. Allow the mold to dry before storing in the press. If you don't, insects that love the taste of the mold in a very short time will take up housekeeping in your press full of moldy bark. Rather than storing moldy bark, I prepare it immediately, and store only clean bark.

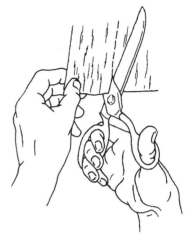

Cutting bark along lenticel lines

When preparing material for weaving, cut off any thick scars or knots that are close to the edges of the sheet of bark. Some pieces will have scars that are just too attractive to cut off. If you want to make folded containers, these scars can be featured and are quite pretty. Leave small scars. When the bark is split, you may find that the under layer of the scar is just fine, and you can use this as a design element in your basket.

Parallel to the lenticel lines, cut strips approximately 2 inches wide. The next step is similar to a technique used in splitting black ash or white oak splints (see illustrations on pages 138–39). Approximately ½ inch from the end of one of the strips, scribe across its width; take care not to cut all the way through the bark. Bend the scored piece so that the layers can be peeled apart. Holding a layer in each hand, anchor the piece of bark between your knees and pull the layers apart. Keep the two halves as even as possible. If one side begins to get thicker than the other, pull harder to the thicker side. Do this with all your strips.

If the sheet you are working with is winter bark and some of the inner bark is on the sap side, you will have to scrape it clean and smooth. Lay the strip of bark on your thigh. Hold the blade of a pocket knife straight on the bark and pull the bark so that the blade scrapes off the inner bark. Do not scrape the blade of your

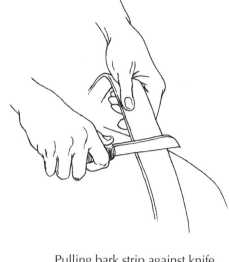

Pulling bark strip against knife.

knife back and forth. This is very time consuming and does not do the job as neatly as pulling the bark against the knife.

You will note that the reverse side of the split strips is covered with a chalky deposit, which you can rub off with a towel. Recently, I have begun treating the bark with mink oil. This makes it very pleasant to touch and enhances its color.

Gauging with your sense of touch, separate the strips according to thickness. You will use the thicker material for spokes; the thinner material, for weavers. For straight plaiting it is most desirable to use material all of the same thickness. You may not always have material of an even thickness on hand when you are first learning how to split bark. If you find you have a lot of very flexible, thin material, use this for diagonal plaiting, such as the Diagonal-Plaited Birch-Bark Pouch on page 101. For straight plaiting, such as the Miniature Plaited Birch-Bark Laundry Basket (page 105), cut all your material ¼ inch wide; for diagonal plaiting, the material should be ⅜ inch wide.

NOTE ON TOOLS

Among the few tools you will need are scissors and a good pocket knife. If you use scissors to cut your material, remember to watch the tip of your scissors. The secret to straight cutting is to watch where you are going, not where you are. You can also use a utility knife and steel rule.

In one of my antique haunts, I was very fortunate to find an old rug wool cutter. This has proven to be an invaluable tool for cutting my bark-weaving material. New cutters, such as the Rigby Cloth Stripping Machine, are available from craft suppliers (see page 151). They are rather expensive, but worth every penny if you plan to do a lot of bark work.

Many basket makers use clothespins to hold the weaving in place during construction, but for miniature baskets like those described here, clothespins can get in the way. I have found that small micro alligator clips (sold at Radio Shack), are easy to work around and hold the weaving securely.

You need little else except something to pack in the weaving and tuck in ends. I like the small Weave Rite tools (available from basketry suppliers); or, you can make a similar tool by rounding the edges of a small screwdriver and grinding the tip smooth.

DIAGONAL-PLAITED BIRCH-BARK POUCH

3½" wide x 2" deep x 7½" high

A wonderful introduction to diagonal plaiting, this pouch will hold a message pad and pencil by your front door, or, if you make a larger one, your garlic in the kitchen. I keep matches in tiny ones. They are also quite pretty with dried flowers tucked inside.

The contrasting colors of the sap side and the outside of the bark are shown to advantage where the weavers are turned back on themselves at the top. If you would like additional interest, weave narrower strips of contrasting colors as overlays on the completed pouch, as done in the sample basket on page 92. The colors are further enhanced by mink oiling the back sides of the bark strips.

MATERIALS

Birch bark: Twelve
⅜"-wide, 24"-long strips

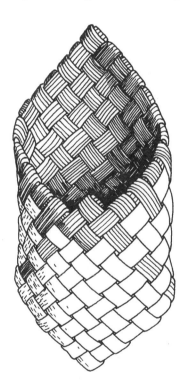

1. Mark the centers of all the strips. Lay two strips across each other at the center marks.

2. Weave the remaining spokes in an under, over fashion *below* these two, keeping all the ends lined up with the first two. The unwoven ends on two sides will be longer than those on the other

two sides. Place clips on the corners to hold the strips in place.
Make sure the spacing between all spokes is even.

STEP 2

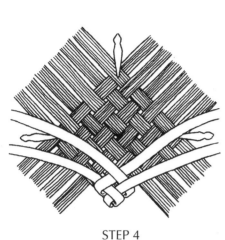

STEP 4

3. Place the woven base from Step 2 in front of you with long
ends at the bottom and short ends above.

4. Fold the two bottom-most corner strips, and weave them over
and under each other.

5. Weave the remaining long ends, five on the left and five on
the right, over and under each other directly on top of the base.
Keep the spacing between spokes even and consistent. Use clips
as needed to hold everything in place.

6. Hold the woven square on its side, so that the bottom point
is facing toward you and the right hand corner is up. Weave the
corner pieces under and over each other.

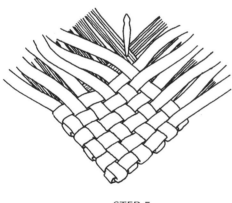

STEP 5

STEP 6

7. Weave all six pieces until there is no more to weave; the right side of the pouch is complete.

8. Repeat Steps 6 and 7 to weave the left side of the pouch.

9. The side of the pouch with the longer ends is the back. Weave these twelve pieces over and under each other until all are woven.

10. Place the pouch with the front facing toward you. Take the middle two pieces, cross them back over each other at the center front, and tuck them into the weaving to hold them in place.

11. On the back side of the pouch, cross the two center top spokes in the same way as you did those on the front; but bring these ends down and around to the front, and use clips or tuck them under the weaving to hold them in place. If the strips are not long enough (which many times they are not) overlap the short end with an extra piece that reaches to the front. This strip is needed for the next step.

12. Fold back *all* the remaining spokes *to the outside*, and tuck them under the weaving.

13. For a hanger, make a loop with an extra strip of bark, and tuck it into the top of the back, weaving the ends down into and under the top row.

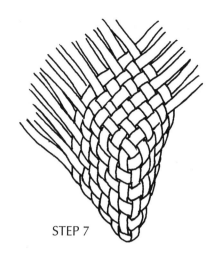

STEP 7

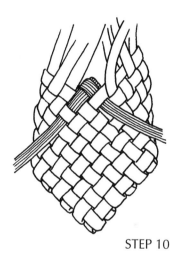

STEP 10

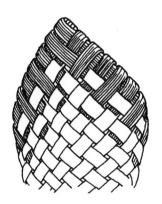

STEPS 11–12

OTHER MATERIALS TO USE WITH BIRCH BARK

The miniature laundry basket (pages 105–7) and the kittenhead basket (pages 109–11) contain other wild materials, in addition to bark. For example, the sides of the laundry basket feature a band of birch bark used sap side out and defined top and bottom by several rows of twined honeysuckle vine. Note how dark the bark looks in the midsection of the sample basket on page 92. One of the wonderful properties of birch bark is the color variation on the back side of the split bark — anything from beige to reddish brown. If you rub this side with a towel or mink oil, the colors become even more intense.

For the honeysuckle vine, I use very fine vine gathered in spring, summer, or fall. I coil the strands to fit in a large canning pot, and boil it for three to four hours. The boiling loosens the bark, so that it peels off easily. You can use #1 round rattan as a substitute, if you have no honeysuckle.

I like to use wisteria or honeysuckle (larger in diameter than that used for twining) for the little bale handles. I like the feel and flexibility of wisteria — plus, it grows in my woods! I gather it in the fall; and as with the honeysuckle, I boil it for about four hours and then peel off the bark. If I am careful when peeling the bark, I can save it to use for cordage or twining in other baskets. The peeled wisteria can be dried and stored, but should be resoaked for about fifteen minutes in warm water when you weave with it.

For the rims of both baskets, I use red-osier dogwood, which I gather in November. I harvest only straight pieces, in various sizes from ¼ inch to 1 inch in diameter. I leave it outside for the entire winter, allowing it to be covered by snow. November-harvested red osier will retain its red bark. I left the bark on for the kittenhead basket rim, but I removed it for the laundry basket. To peel red osier, put a piece across your thigh, and pressing a knife against it with the blade at a slight angle, pull the withe of dogwood between your leg and the knife so that the bark comes off. Remember, move only the dogwood; do not move the knife. (Wear heavy jeans or cover your leg with a piece of leather, so that you don't cut yourself.)

After the red outer bark is removed, scrape the withe to remove the green inner bark and expose the shiny, white wood beneath. To get two half-round pieces for a rim, you will have to split this withe in half lengthwise. Start the split with your knife until you have two ends to grasp. Hold the withe tightly between your knees to keep it under control, and continue the split. Pull harder to the thicker side, to keep the split on center.

To prevent the dogwood from kinking when it is wrapped around the basket, you can break down the fibers by rolling the piece in the palm of your hand and pushing against it with your thumb.

To lash the rims to my baskets, I use split cedar root, or, as in the sample baskets, black ash. Birch is not good for lashing, as it has a tendency to split on the lenticel lines when cut this narrow.

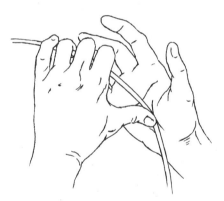

Bending a withe of red-osier dogwood.

MINIATURE PLAITED BIRCH-BARK LANDRY BASKET

3¼" wide x 4¾" long x 2⅞" high

This is a simple straight-plaited basket (shown on color page 92) that can be used to store teabags or a pair of salt-and-pepper shakers, or just as a pretty accent piece among your collectibles. As with all patterns, it is best to read the entire instructions before starting this project.

1. Mark the centers on the back of each bark strip. These marks will be on the inside of your basket.

2. Lay out the nine 11-inch verticals side by side. Anchor their ends with a heavy object (a book, for instance).

3. Using one of the 13-inch strips, weave through the centers of the 11-inch strips, going over and under adjoining spokes all the way across. Weave a 7-inch filler spoke above and below the center 13-inch spoke. Weave a 13-inch spoke above and below the 7-inch filler spokes. Continue this pattern until you have used all five 13-inch strips and all four 7-inch fillers. Make sure the

MATERIALS

Birch bark:
> nine ¼"-wide, 11" strips (spokes)

> five ¼"-wide, 13" strips (spokes)

> four ¼"-wide, 7" strips (fillers)

> six ¼"-wide, 15" strips (weavers)

> three ³⁄₁₆"-wide, 15" strips (center weavers)

Very fine, peeled honeysuckle vine (or #1 round rattan):
> enough to weave about 30' (sides)

Peeled wisteria or honeysuckle:
> two ⅛"-diameter, 6" long pieces (handles)

Peeled red-osier dogwood:
> two ¼"-wide, 15" long, half-round pieces (rim)

Split black ash or cedar root:
> enough ⅛"-wide to lash rim (46–48 inches)

nine 11-inch strips are evenly spaced, approximately ¼ inch apart. Clip the corners to hold everything in place.

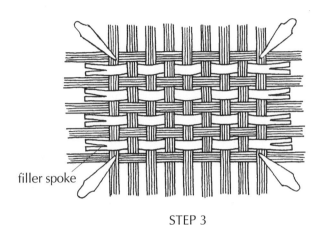

filler spoke

STEP 3

4. Turn the base over. Split the ends of the filler pieces in half vertically. Fold them back over the base, and tuck them under the second spoke.

5. Turn the base back over, so that the wrong side faces up. Bend all the spokes up along the edge of the base. Begin weaving the sides. Using ¼-inch strips approximately 15 inches long, weave three rows of start-and-stop, under-and-over weaving. **To weave start-and-stop fashion,** each row of weaving ends when a complete round of the basket has been made. Always start a weaver on top of a spoke and finish it behind a spoke, so it will be hidden; overlap the beginning and end for four spokes. Be sure that on each row you are weaving over the spokes that you wove under on the row below and vice versa. If you find a mistake, look for a place where you have gone under or over two adjoining spokes. Keep the spokes straight, and be careful not to pull in the corners too tightly, as this will cause the sides to draw in. The first three rows of the sides are the most difficult.

6. Using three pieces of the honeysuckle vine (or the #1 round rattan) do three rows of triple weave. To triple weave, start with one piece of honeysuckle coming out from between each of three adjoining spokes. Beginning with the vine on the far left (A), go over two spokes, behind one spoke, and out to the right. Do the same with the next weaver (B). Continue in this manner until you have completed three rows. Clip the ends of the weavers, leaving about ½ inch on the inside of the basket.

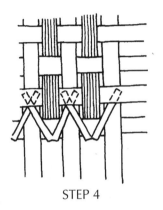

STEP 4

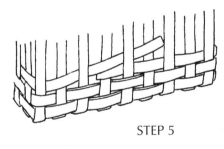

STEP 5

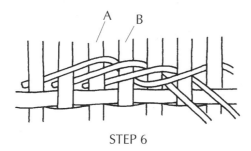

STEP 6

7. Weave three more rows of start-and-stop weaving *with the sap side of the bark out.* This creates the dark band in the center of the basket sides.

8. Weave three more rows of triple weave with the honeysuckle vine, as in Step 6.

9. Weave three final rows of start-and-stop weaving with ¼-inch bark, white side out.

10. Cut *outside* spokes to a length suitable for tucking under the third from the top row of weaving on the inside (about 1 inch). Use a small Weave Rite to help you tuck in the spokes. Cut the remaining (inside) spokes flush with the top of the basket.

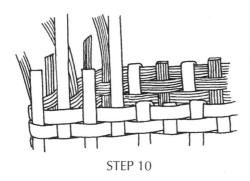

STEP 10

11. Taper both ends of the handle pieces with your knife, and push them into the ends of the basket, with one spoke between them, as shown in the completed basket. They should extend about 1½ inches into the basket.

12. Measure the circumference of your basket, and add about 2 inches extra for an overlap. Cut one of the half-round pieces this length for the outside rim; the inside rim is usually about 1 inch shorter. To make the overlap, shave the topside of one end and the underside of the other end. Put both inner and outer rims in position, placing the joins on opposite sides of the basket. Anchor the rims with clothespins.

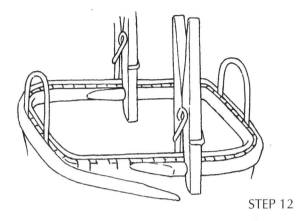

STEP 12

13. Lay the lasher between the outside rim and the last row of weaving. Bring it down behind the inside rim, between two spokes, and to the outside. Lash the entire rim, going between each spoke and under the last row of weaving.

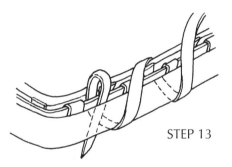

STEP 13

14. For the last stitch of lashing, rather than coming to the outside, go up behind the inside rim, then back under the last stitch.

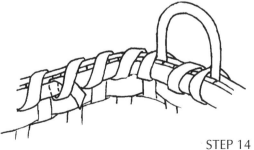

STEP 14

KITTENHEAD BIRCH-BARK BASKET

4¾" diameter x 3" high

This charming little basket (shown on color page 92) takes its name from its base, which resembles the top of a kitten's head. The Shakers, who developed the kittenhead basket, worked on a wooden mold to create the little triangles that represent the kitten's ears. This technique of creating a kittenhead without a mold was taught to me by my friend Judith Olney. It is quite easy to do, but very impressive when completed. The more rows you weave with the base flat on the table, the more exaggerated the ears.

MATERIALS

Birch bark:
>fourteen ¼" wide, 14"-long strips (spokes)

>thirteen ¼" wide, 17–18"-long strips (weavers)

Peeled wisteria vine:
>two ⅛" diameter, 6" long pieces (handles)

Red-osier dogwood:
>two ¼" wide, 16"-long, half-round pieces, one peeled (outer rim) and one unpeeled (inner rim)

Split black ash or split cedar root:
>enough ⅛" wide to lash rim (48–50 inches)

1. Mark the centers of all spokes on the wrong side (the side you have chosen for the inside of your basket).

2. Lay seven spokes down in front of you vertically, with the center marks aligned.

3. Weave one of the remaining seven spokes under and over horizontally through these verticals at the center. Weave the remaining six, three above and three below the first horizontal. When all fourteen spokes are woven together, make sure the spaces between the spokes are even little squares, not rectangles. The base should measure approximately 2 ½" x 2½". Use clips to hold the corners in place.

STEP 3

4. This is the step that forms the distinctive shape. With the wrong side facing up, leave the base *flat* on the table. Begin the first row of start-and-stop weaving (see Step 5, page 106) by starting over a spoke. Weave in an under one, over one pattern. When you get to a corner, pull your weaver very tightly around it, so that the corner spokes literally stand up. Complete the row of weaving by overlapping the ends of the weavers for four spokes; always bury your weaver end under a spoke.

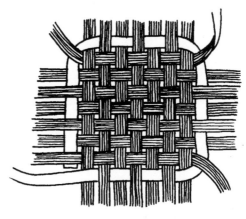

STEP 4

5. Weave one more row with the wrong side facing up, again pulling tightly around the corners.

6. Turn the base over so that the outside of the basket faces up. Leaving the base *flat* on the table, weave two more rows, pulling the weavers tightly at the corners as before, while at the same time "sunbursting" the spokes.

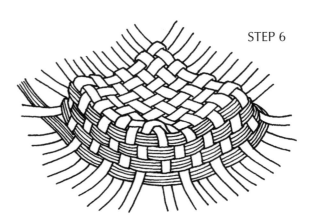

STEP 6

7. You will now weave with your spokes going upright. Note that the first four rows of weaving are loose on the corners; this is to be expected. Continue weaving until you have completed about seven rows, using lots of clips to hold your weaving in the desired shape.

8. Go back and tighten up your original weaving. This is a time-consuming step, but necessary for a finished look and a structurally sound basket. You must also continue to encourage the corners to protrude beyond the base of the basket by using your thumbs to push up the center of the basket, while gently pushing the little ears down from the inside.

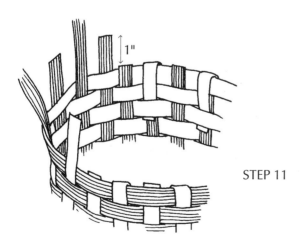

STEP 8

9. Continue weaving until you have completed thirteen rows. The thirteenth row is a false rim — a row that will be buried under the half-round rim. When weaving the last three rows, you may wish to pull your weaving a little tighter than in the previous rows. This creates a nice "potbelly" look.

10. Pack down all the weaving so there are no gaps between the rows.

11. Cut the *outside* spokes to a length long enough to tuck under two rows of weaving on the inside of the basket (about 1 inch). Bend these spokes over the top row toward the inside, and tuck them under two rows below. When all of the outside spokes have been woven to the inside, cut the remaining spokes flush with the top of the basket.

1"

STEP 11

12. Follow Steps 11–14, pages 107–8, to complete the handles, rims, and lashing of your basket.

VINES AND BASKET GARDENING

DORIS MESSICK

asketry combines two of my loves — nature and making things by hand. Since my childhood, the woods have been a favorite place for me, and I still find the wonders of nature never-ending. While others collect jewelry or fancy glassware, I bring home treasures of nature — a discarded bird's or hornets' nest, a vine or tree trunk with wonderful twists and turns. When I am traveling, my pictures are not of fancy buildings or memorials but of holes in trees and twisted trunks. To me, these are the world's wonders.

Creating things with my own hands is my other passion. When I see an object I like, I have to try to make it — better, of course. One lifetime is not nearly enough to try everything with which I want to experiment. For awhile, my favorite medium was clay. It provides a legitimate excuse to play, get dirty, and make a mess, like being a child again. In the end, if all goes well, you will have created a handsome object. Then, I discovered basketry! As with pottery, it allows you to play and make a mess, and beautiful objects emerge. Unlike pottery, however, you don't have to wait for the final result — no firing in the kiln, no breakage, and no uncertain glazing. The rewards are immediate. I was hooked with the creation of my very first basket.

The more involved in basketry I became, the more dissatisfied I was with the materials I was purchasing. At that time, I had to rely on mail-ordered supplies and could not therefore judge the quality before purchase. Basketry materials made expensive kindling. I was thrilled when I discovered that I could make wonderful baskets from the treasures I found in the woods. Purchased wooden hoops could not compare with the magically twisted vine handles I unearthed in my explorations. My old love, a walk in the woods, was now a necessity.

My "discovery" was, in fact, nothing new. Historically, baskets were made with available materials, which might be anything from grasses to trees. The style and technique of basketry in any area depended on what grew there. Coiling, for instance, was prevalent where only grasses, rushes, and sedges grew. Wood-splint and bark basket styles were determined by the kind of trees indigenous to the area. Even the quality of the materials was affected by the location. White oak splints, for example, vary according to the conditions under which the tree grew. On Maryland's Eastern Shore, where I live, baskets were created strictly for use as heavy-duty farm baskets or eel pots. They looked nothing like the Appalachian baskets constructed of thin, flexible white oak splints. How could they, when the good white oak trees grow on the north side of a mountain, yet the highest spot in our county is only 34 feet above sea level?

BASKETRY MATERIALS FROM NATURE

Fall and spring are the best times to gather many basketry materials. Weather is usually at its best, and the bug and unwanted animal populations are low. The lack of foliage means not only that you can spot the vines you want more easily, but also that you will have no leaves to strip. If you are planning to remove the bark, you will find it is easiest to do in the spring right after the sap rises; at that point, no boiling is necessary. Even with these advantages of fall and spring gathering, however, it's possible to collect your materials year round, though perhaps a bit more difficult and not as pleasant.

Before you weave with any hand-gathered natural materials, you must prepare them so that they won't shrink after use and weaken the structure of your completed basket. Most materials must be allowed to sit at least several days, at which time you have two options. You can form the framework while the vine is still fresh and pliable, or you can dry the material completely and store it for future use. If you choose the second option, you will have to soak the vine before using it. Large garbage cans (at least 30 gallons) work well for this purpose. The length of time required for soaking varies with the water temperature as well as with the size and type of vine. Stripped vines soak up water faster than those with bark. Heavy vines may take several days to become flexible, whereas weavers may require only an hour or overnight at the most. The vine will deteriorate if you soak it too long, so keep checking to see if it has become flexible enough to use. I try to have several projects underway at the same time, so I'm not held up waiting for materials to become pliable.

VINES

Wisteria, honeysuckle, kudzu, grape, Virginia creeper, and akebia are the vines I use the most, because they are available to me in the Mid-Atlantic region; other parts of the country have other interesting vines, just waiting to be tried. Supplejack (*Berchemia* spp.), which grows in the South, is actually not very supple, but it makes a delightful, contorted framework with a smooth gray-green bark. Bittersweet (*Celastrus* spp.) has similar characteristics, but its bark is bumpy, gray, and speckled. Neither supplejack nor bittersweet weaves well. Kiwi (*Actinidia* spp.) is reputed to be a great basket material. Finding what fits your needs just takes experimentation. If it looks interesting, try it and see what it will do.

Wisteria (*Wisteria floribunda*)

Wisteria. If I could have just one basketry plant, it would be wisteria. I have yet to find a technique that can't be done with some part of the wisteria vine. The large upper growth, with its wonderful twists and turns formed by its growth around trees and other obstacles, is my favorite for framework. The long ground runners, which are its means of propagation, are the most flexible of the large weavers. Half-inch ground runners can be used with no splitting. I have found no other plant that provides weavers of this caliber. Even the bark of wisteria is a valued commodity, for although it is thin, it is extremely strong and makes a wonderful wrapping material. When I want to use the vine, however, I do not strip off the bark: a stripped wisteria vine is usually hairy and weak. I find it perfect to use just as Nature grew it.

Wisteria is best harvested where it has escaped into the wild. Cultivated plants do not get as contorted. In the center of my neighbors' front yard is a wisteria that is so carefully pruned I wouldn't recognize it if it didn't bloom — no basketry materials there. If a wisteria is growing on a manicured lawn, its runners will have been ruined by the lawn mower.

Honeysuckle. After wisteria, honeysuckle is next on my

preferred list. It is usually found growing in areas that have been cultivated and then neglected. It thrives along rows between fields and lanes, and in hedges and bushes. You'll find it along the edge of woods, but it needs light too much to grow in deep woods. Because honeysuckle chokes out other less aggressive plants, many people are more than willing to let you harvest, and in fact, will call you if they know you want it.

Most basket makers like to strip honeysuckle bark, as it spirals on the vine and sheds constantly unless removed. Spring is therefore the best time to gather it, as the rising sap makes bark removal easy. If you collect it at other times, you will have to boil it to remove the bark. The resulting vine is smooth, hard, and light in color; it takes dye well.

If you don't mind boiling the vine, you may find it easier to gather in the winter than in spring, because it is more visible then. Honeysuckle vines retain some of their leaves, making the light-colored vine readily seen among the bare branches. This is especially true of the heavier vines growing under small ones, which hide them in the summer. If the ground is moist but not frozen, you will be able to pull up the roots in winter. These, too, are excellent additions to any basket.

Kudzu. In the 1930s, kudzu was imported from Japan for erosion control in the South. It is what I call a beginner vine, as it is so easy to use. Fast-growing and strong, kudzu is used in Japan as cattle feed, medicine, food, drink, paper, and fabric. Unfortunately, the extraordinary toughness of kudzu vines causes them to clog the machinery of our mechanized society, and kudzu is thus considered more of a weed than a useful plant in the United States. It just *grows* — covering trees, houses, and whatever else is in its path.

The upper growth is similar in appearance to wisteria, though not as woody or strong. It is fine for framework on a decorative piece, but is not as durable as you would expect of a vine of its size. The bark, which is practically rip-proof, varies in thickness with the size of the vine; it can be used as weavers, for wrapping, or even for cordage. My favorite parts, though, are the ground runners, which just go on and on. If used whole, they kink, but when split, they are wonderfully flexible. There is none of the breakage or cracking that you get with many vines.

Grapevine. The first vine everyone thinks of in relation to baskets is grapevine. I love its delightful tendrils, which I have just recently started using for free-form miniatures. Grapevines can be wild, cultivated, or escaped. They tend to be straighter than other vines, thus lending themselves to more traditional shapes. It is most suitable for use as framework. With the exception of muscadine vines, grapevine is not very flexible and makes poor weavers, even in the smaller diameters.

Although I love the bark, I always boil and strip any grapevine I use. Prone to insects, it is even more susceptible when the bark is left on. The boiling kills any eggs within the vine that could hatch later.

Muscadine (*Vitis rotundifolia*), which grows in warm climates only (to Zone 6), is usable in wickerwork, where there are no sharp bends. Its aerial roots are small but quite decorative. Beginners find the tendrils frustrating, as they catch on everything.

Virginia creeper, Woodbine. Common throughout much of the U.S., Virginia creeper is not very strong. It appears to do best when used fairly fresh, but once dry, it never regains full flexibility. As with kudzu, the long ground runners are the preferred weavers; the tiny tendrils add a lot.

Akebia. A Japanese import, akebia can be used as harvested or with the bark stripped. Boiled, stripped akebia can be dyed, but I prefer to use it natural. A skinny version of kudzu, this vine is excellent for weaving miniature baskets or for starting larger baskets where small weavers work best.

Virginia creeper
(*Parthenocissus quinquefolia*)

BARKS

Barks are best harvested in the spring when the sap is rising, as this is the only time of the year when they will come off easily. Barks are a good source of flat material. It's easier, and also conserves trees, to look for branches that have been pruned or blown down in a storm. Small weed trees in ditches are also good sources. Simply score the bark lengthwise and around the circumference of the branch at the top and bottom, and then peel it off. Keep in mind, however that if you girdle a tree trunk, the tree will die. If the outer bark is stiff, remove it by flexing it until you can peel it off. Hickory and elm, which produce a material much like leather, are my favorites.

OTHER MATERIALS

Saplings, abundant in ditches, make good round weavers. Just about any small tree that is flexible can be used. Bush-type willows are great. Don't be tempted by weeping willows, however; though wonderful when fresh, they become brittle when dry. Red-osier dogwoods give great color.

When I travel in the South, I look for favorites like palm inflorescences, Spanish moss, and philodendron sheaths, all of which make excellent weavers. Yard services are great sources for these materials. What is a treasure to a basket maker is rubbish to maintenance services, which usually have to pay to dispose of clippings. You may even be able to rescue materials from brush dumps.

SOME COLLECTING TIPS

Collecting is reasonably safe, but be aware of possible dangers, such as poisonous plants and unwelcome animals. Learn to recognize poisonous plants that grow in your area. The two most common are poison ivy and poison oak. The old childhood saying — "Leaves of three, let it be" — is good advice at the time of year when the leaves are out, but for wintertime collecting, you should learn to recognize the white berries and the hairy stems going up a tree. The best precaution is not to touch anything that you can't identify — including those wonderful roots that some construction crew unearthed. Remember that the toxins in the roots are concentrated and therefore much more potent. Wear gloves and wash thoroughly as soon as you return home.

Make noise while collecting. Snakes and other animals avoid confrontation, if at all possible. Trouble comes only when they feel threatened or are cornered.

The most effective preventives against insect bites that I've found are to avoid collecting in hot weather whenever possible and to take a thorough shower, scrubbing all cracks and crevices, as soon as you return. If you think you may encounter problems, wear long sleeves, long pants, and insect repellent. A netted hat will be welcome if the bugs are really bad. Deer ticks have become a threat that we can't ignore, especially in some locations. Pull your socks over your pants legs and use repellent. Check your clothing and your skin when you come in from fields and woods. Chiggers like hot, dry conditions. Dust powdered sulphur around your ankles and waist to discourage attacks, and don't sit on rotten wood.

BASKET GARDENING

Basket gardening can add a new dimension to your basketry. If you grow your own materials, they can be collected in your own backyard whenever you need them, no matter what the weather. You may even be able to grow materials that are not naturally available in your area. Plant even those materials that do grow locally, because just knowing they are right there in your garden if you need them can give you a great sense of security.

Wisteria was the beginning of my basketry garden. Not only is it my favorite basketry material, it also has beautiful purple blooms. As mentioned earlier, it needs to be planted in an area where it can grow wild. To increase my stand of wisteria and ensure my supply, I cut off sections with large roots that appear along the runners every few feet and plant them. Wisteria seems to produce the best runners when planted in a lightly wooded area where the main plant gets some sun; the runners grow vigorously as they seek out open areas. Wisteria grows well in full sun, too, but it does not produce the desired long runners.

These same growing conditions work for honeysuckle, bittersweet, and akebia. Do *not* plant kudzu — it just might grow! It is sold through some catalogs as ground cover, but eradication is almost impossible, once it is established. In some states, planting kudzu is against the law. It appears to be increasingly freeze resistant; I have seen healthy stands as far north as Delaware.

Basket willows are a great crop. You can purchase cuttings or harvest your own from wild willows. I like to plant as great a variety as possible, so that I have a mixture of colors for my baskets. My garden includes several varieties of basket willow, creek willow, and pussy willow. A new Japanese variety of pussy willow has the contortions of a wisteria and miniature catkins that stay on, even through soaking.

I take 12-inch cuttings, at least a pencil's width thick; thicker is better. I cut the base at a slant and the top straight across, so I can identify which end to plant. Before planting the cuttings, I

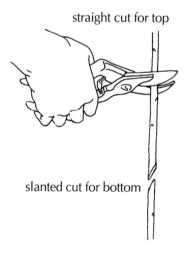

straight cut for top

slanted cut for bottom

Basket willow cutting

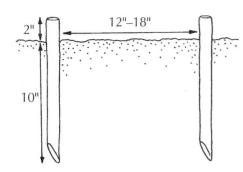

Basket willow cuttings
inserted in soil

Yucca

work the soil until it is loose and weed-free. If you have clay soil, lighten it by adding some sand and/or compost. I push the slanted ends of the cuttings into the soil 12 to 18 inches apart and 10 inches deep, with 2 inches above the surface. Willows do not compete well with weeds (and *I* don't weed well), so I find it is important to mulch heavily. After the second year, weeding will be no problem, as the willow patch will be full of willow roots. Each cutting produces at least two withes (long stems) the first year. The length, ranging from 6 to 12 feet, depends on growing conditions, as well as the species.

Willow can be harvested any time after frost, but I wait until late winter, just before the catkins come out completely, because I like to incorporate them into my baskets. I cut the willows back to the first or second bud on each stem every year. Each cut stem will produce two more withes the following year. When harvesting, I cut off the bottom 12 inches of each withe and push it back in the ground to start a new patch. If the withe is extra thick, I make more than one cutting. The thinner, more flexible tops are my basketry materials. (For additional information about growing willow, see pages 18–19.)

Osier dogwood can be propagated the same way as willows. It also comes in several varieties that give great color. I have purchased a red-twig Japanese variety that stays red all year, as well as a yellow-twig variety. Friends have sent me cuttings, and I have collected some myself. Although the osier dogwoods are not native to our area, my garden crop does well. As with willows, harvest in cold weather for the best color.

Yuccas edge my garden. I encourage my friends to use them for their own landscaping, even providing the plants when I have extras. (Of course, in such cases, I request harvesting rights!) The leaves are unbelievably strong. I used them at first as weavers, and now use them as spokes, too. They work equally well whole, flat, or split, twisted together in bunches or corded. Harvest yucca leaves only from the bottom. Pull the leaf out and down from the main stalk, spiraling around as you pull, so you don't damage the base. As long as you don't take the center leaf core, you won't hurt the plant. As new leaves grow, the ones at the base naturally die. Harvesting is simply grooming the plant.

Every garden needs flowers. Select yours carefully, and they will serve a dual purpose. You can beautify your yard and, at the same time, reap benefits for your basketry. The leaves of many common annuals, perennials, and bulbs make great weavers. Look for any plants with long leaves that flourish in your area. Choose those with obvious veins, as they are stronger. After you pick the leaves, spread them out to dry to prevent rot. Fresh leaves have too much moisture to be used successfully. Once dry, they must be briefly soaked to regain flexibility before weaving. Some may disintegrate at this point, but if they are still strong when dampened or soaked, go ahead and use them.

The leaves of daylilies (*Hemerocallis* spp.) are one of the most commonly used basketry materials. To increase their strength, they are usually bunched together, twisted, corded, or even spun by hand or with a wheel. Collect at different times of the season to get a variety of colors. Dry leaves in the shade to preserve colors, or use the sun to bleach leaves. Most garden catalogs carry dozens of *Hemerocallis* cultivars.

The Iris Family is another good source. As well as iris, this family includes gladiolus, watsonia, and tritonia. If you plant them all, you will have quite a variety of leaf colors. I'm particularly fond of the watsonia leaf, which dries a rich mahogany brown with a yellow rib. Watsonias are not winter hardy (Zone 7) and in cold climates need to be dug up each year. In Maryland, we are borderline, but heavy mulching usually works.

Daffodils and red-hot-pokers are also good choices. You may have others already growing in your garden.

Virginia creeper is a bonus garden plant. In the wild, the runners of this vine are difficult to harvest, as they become tangled with other plants. In a well-mulched garden, however, Virginia creeper provides bountiful long runners all year long. I planted it in my first basket garden, and it took over; all subsequent garden plots have had naturally occurring creeper. It is one plant you know will grow. It should be frequently harvested.

Daylily

COLLECTING NATURAL MATERIALS
NATURAL BASKETRY GATHERING GUIDE

COMMON NAME *BOTANICAL NAME*	CHARACTERISTICS	PREPARATION TIPS	USES
Vines			
Akebia *Akebia quinata*	Fast-growing, thin-diameter vine from Japan. Five small, round leaves around single stem. Small, purple, 1-inch-long flower in spring. Very flexible.	Use with or without bark.	Excellent for miniatures and tight places, such as basket beginnings.
Grapevine *Vitis* spp.	Many varieties, both domestic and wild. Smooth or rough bark with tendrils. In the South, smooth-barked muscadine has wonderful aerial roots. Moderate to poor flexibility.	Harvest after frost so that grape production is not hurt. Form vine when fresh, or soak several days to restore flexibility. *Rough bark:* Boil several hours to remove bark and kill eggs of powder post beetles and other insects. *Smooth bark (muscadine):* You can leave the bark on this more flexible variety.	Use mostly for framework.
Honeysuckle *Lonicera japonica*	Widespread woody vine with wonderful twists and turns. Simple oval leaves grow opposite one another on stems. Small, fragrant, white or yellow flowers. Black berries. Loose, spiraling bark.	May be dried and then resoaked for use. Peel off bark when green; boiling makes this process easier.	Thick vines make good framework. Use long thin runners as weavers; works best with wicker-type technique, as it tends to crack when bent sharply.
Kudzu *Pueraria lobata*	Known as "the vine that covers the South." Large, fast-growing, climbing vine imported from Asia. Three large-lobed leaves.	Bark is usually left on for strength. The bark itself, however, may be used for weavers or cordage, if removed after boiling.	Use large heavy vines for framework. Long ground runners make excellent large weavers when split before use.
Virginia creeper, Woodbine *Parthenocissus quinquefolia*	Five-leafed creeping vine with tiny tendrils. Blue fruits.	Best used fresh after several days of shrinkage.	Long runners used as weavers.

COMMON NAME BOTANICAL NAME	CHARACTERISTICS	PREPARATION TIPS	USES
Wisteria *Wisteria floribunda*	Large, climbing vine with pea-shaped flowers	Do not strip bark from vines.	Heavy vines used as framework. Long ground runners make wonderful weavers.
Marsh Plants	Grow in ditches or other wet areas	Collect when upper tips become brown. Because shrinkage in these plants is excessive, dry them first and then moisten them until flexible for use.	Core for coiling. As weavers, should be twisted or corded for strength.
Rushes *Juncus* spp.	Round stems of various lengths and thicknesses, depending on species		
Sedges *Carex* spp.	Triangular stem of various lengths and thicknesses, depending on species		
Cattail *Typha* spp.	Both narrow and broad leaf, depending on species. Strongest grow in fresh water.		Use leaf.
Shrubs		Collect long *withes* (branches) in dormant stage.	Framework or weavers, depending on thickness and flexibility. Great spokes or fill for random weave.
Basket willow *Salix purpurea* S. *viminalis* and others		Allow 1 week for shrinkage. If dry, soak several days. Mellow overnight in wet towels.	
Pussy willow *Salix caprea, S. discolor,* and others		Catkins will stay on branches if they are harvested before catkins erupt.	
Wild willow	Many varieties and colors		
Red-osier dogwood *Cornus sericea*	Bright red stems in winter		
Leaves			
Yucca *Yucca* spp.	Strong leaves	Dry and resoak before using.	Weavers or soft spokes. Split leaves may be twisted or woven flat.

COMMON NAME BOTANICAL NAME	CHARACTERISTICS	PREPARATION TIPS	USES
Palm (Various spp.)	A variety of tropical plants that grow in warm climates, including the Southern states; also available in greenhouses. Look for palmetto, a weed plant that grows low, for easy harvesting; it grows as far north as North Carolina.	Best used while still green, after several days shrinkage.	Weavers
Ornamental grasses (Various spp.)	Look for long-leaf varieties with prominent ribs for strength.		Weavers
Bulbs and Perennials			
Bulbs (Various spp.)		Collect leaves after bloom. (Note: These are the food collectors for the following year's blossoms; if you pick them before they are completely withered, your bulbs will not blossom the following spring.) Dry on screens or hang in small bunches to prevent rot. Resoak before use.	Cord or twist leaves together for strength and bulk.
Daylilies *Hemerocallis* spp.	Leaf color changes after frost.		
Gladiolus *Gladiolus* x *hortulanus*			
Bugle lily *Watsonia* spp.			
Tritonia *Tritonia* spp.			

RANDOM-WEAVE MARKET BASKET OF HONEYSUCKLE VINE

Random weaving is a great project for beginners. If you learn just a few simple basics, you can't fail. Because you needn't worry about materials shrinking — tight weaving is not characteristic of this style — you can gather and weave all at the same time. For me, it's a quick, fun, and relaxing project to do at the end of the day. The weaving technique consists simply of making a framework and filling in the spaces.

It is easiest to start with a long vine, such as honeysuckle, that is flexible enough to weave with. Use fresh, or boil to remove the bark. The basket shown on page 93 is of honeysuckle, with bark removed after boiling.

The only tools you will need are a pair of sturdy garden clippers and some twist ties.

MATERIALS

Bundle of honeysuckle vines

STEP 1

1. With one long, continuous piece of vine form two large hoops, at right angles to each other. The use of one vine forms a natural connection between the hoops that holds them together.

2. Reinforce these hoops with at least two more loosely twisted vines around the original hoops. Keep all vines flowing in the same direction as the original around the frame.

STEP 2

3. Add new vines as needed; always starting at the rim. Secure these vines by twisting several times in the same direction as the other vines that form the hoop. As you fill in the framework, keep imagining a watermelon rests in the basket, contained by the weaving.

4. Form the basket bottom with a vine beginning in the center of the horizontal hoop and moving toward the bottom framework of the basket (the lower part of the handle). Wrap around the bottom framework and continue around the other side of the basket to the opposite rim. At this point, and each time you come to the rim, go completely around it (do *not* just loop over it) to lock the weaver in place and make the vine lie smoothly along the top of the basket. It is important to do this correctly, or the wrapping will pop up and look loose and poorly woven.

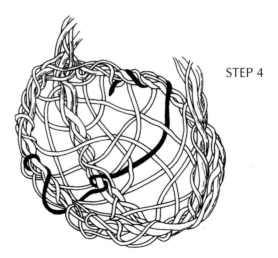

STEP 4

5. Continue going randomly from side to side in different directions until the basket shape is defined by at least four to six vines. Use twist-ties to hold vines in place where they cross one another. Don't forget to wrap completely around the rim each and every time you reach it.

As you weave remember that invisible watermelon in the center — go *around*, not *through* it. When you have several vines, begin to weave under and over them with the new ones. New weavers no longer need to go from rim to rim, but in any direction required to define the space. Go over vines that are protruding and under those that need pushing out. The under-over weaving locks the vines in place and firms up the shape. The diagram illustrates the fastest way to secure the vines, but not the only one. Remove twist-ties when framework is secure.

Continue weaving until the basket is sturdy and filled to your liking. A randomly woven basket can be open and airy or filled in. I filled in every single hole of my first one. Succeeding ones, however, became open and free. Currently, I like to add materials just until the basket is nestlike in appearance.

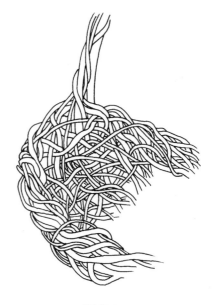

STEP 5

TIPS

❦ No specific pattern is needed, but I like to arrange the vines so they appear to be flowing in the same direction.

❦ Start and end all vines on the rim, so the ends can be tucked in.

❦ As the basket develops, the handle often appears too small in proportion to the rest of the basket. If this happens, simply bring another vine up over the handle and weave it in with the others.

RANDOM-WEAVE VARIATION: A NEST

My favorite random-weave variation is a nestlike basket. Start with a single hoop of a fairly straight vine, such as wisteria. Instead of thinking of a watermelon nestled in the basket, in this case imagine making a container for a ball, and make a sphere-shaped loop of vine between opposite sides of the rim. Wrap more vine completely around the rim, and then make a second matching loop. Continue wrapping vine around the rim and make one more hoop. Secure this shape with twist ties, and then begin the weaving. To increase the basket's nestlike appearance, fill it in completely with withes of willow and red- and yellow-osier dogwood. Any twigs 3 feet in length or longer are usable. Once you have a thick, sturdy nest, weave an outside layer in a more regular, spiraling pattern. Pussy willows are an effective addition.

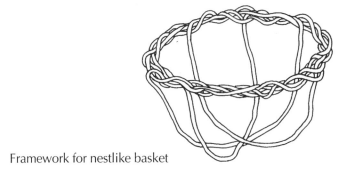

Framework for nestlike basket

VINE-GATHERING BASKET WITH RIB CONSTRUCTION

An endless variety of baskets — traditional through sculptural — have rib construction. Appalachian-style egg or melon baskets are the most commonly known. I find that this technique is particularly suited to vines and use it extensively. A simple gathering basket (shown on color page 93) is a good way to explore rib construction.

All materials must be collected at least five to seven days in advance to allow time for shrinkage. It is fun to weave baskets with freshly picked materials, which you can do for random-weave baskets. For other weaves, however, it is not at all rewarding in the long run, as fresh-woven materials dry loose and wobbly. Frames are easiest made with fresh vines that have dried at least several days before use; the thicker the vine, the longer the drying period that is needed. Soak materials that have been collected earlier and dried.

The thickness of the vine should determine the size of the basket. A large basket made from a skinny vine will look out of proportion.

In addition to your garden clippers, you will also need some strong twine or waxed cord, preferably in a color that blends with the vines being used.

MATERIALS

Sturdy vines for framework

Flexible weaving materials, such as leaves, barks, small vines, marsh grasses, palm inflorescences, and philo-dendron sheaths

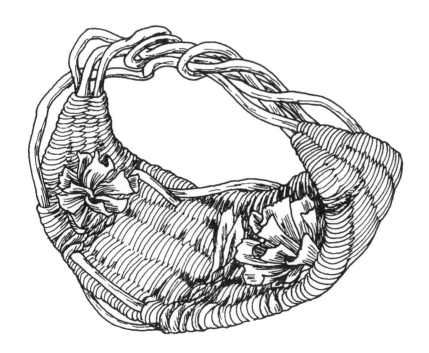

1. Use two intersecting hoops to start this basket. For each hoop, loosely twist together at least three lengths of vine. It is important to twist the vines loosely, so that later, when you weave across the frame, you will have room to slip the weavers around only one or two of the framing vines, thus leaving at least one vine exposed. The beauty of the vines in the framework is lost if the weavers cover them completely.

2. Adjust the frame so that the hoops are connected only at the top and spread apart at the bottom. Tie a stick or piece of vine across the bottom of the hoops to hold them the desired distance apart. This is all the frame will need.

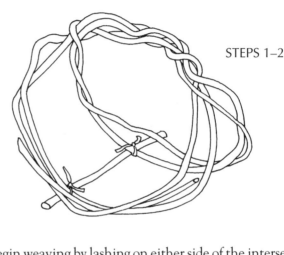

STEPS 1–2

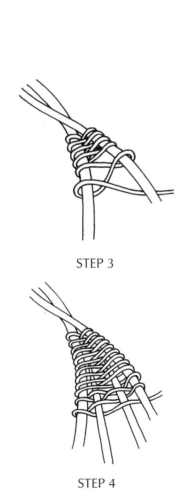

STEP 3

STEP 4

3. Begin weaving by lashing on either side of the intersection of the two hoops. I like to use a strong, skinny, flexible vine for this lashing. Hold one end of the lashing vine down along one of the sides, and begin to do a figure eight (cover the end as you weave). Remember do *not* cover all the vines that make up the framework; instead, select one from each side of the "V" to weave around. If you stop to analyze the figure-eight lashing technique, you will realize you are simply weaving over and under.

4. Lash both sides until the holes under both sides of the center crossing are approximately ¼ inch in diameter. These holes will hold your ribs. For the ribs, use vine that is straighter and just slightly thinner than that used for framework. Cut one end on a diagonal, and insert it in one of the holes. Holding the basket upside down, bring the first rib to the hole in the lashing on the opposite side. Adjust to give the desired length. Cut this end of the rib on the diagonal, too, and insert it in the opening. Repeat this process for the second rib, using remaining holes.

5. Continue weaving and include these ribs in the established over, under pattern.

6. At the point where you begin adding ribs (or within the next few inches, if you wish), add yucca "flowers" as accents; dracena leaves will work as well. To make these flowerlike decorations, gather together a bunch of soaked leaves at the base (wide) end, and tie them tightly; the tighter you tie, the prettier the flower. Waxed cord or waxed dental floss makes it easy to get a firm tie. Spread the leaf bases out to form petals, and position on basket. They look best tucked in behind a vine, as though growing out from it. Do *not* place flowers on a rim or on the outside of the basket; no matter what you do, they will stick out and look awkward. When you get them positioned the way you want them, tie them in place. The remainder of the leaves will be used as weavers.

7. Split the leaves lengthwise to form strips approximately ¼ inch wide. Separate the strips into manageable groups, twist two to four pieces together, and weave them in. Work with one group at a time. I often use the twining technique for groups of leaves. To twine, work with two weavers or groups of weavers at a time. Twining is simply a twist of two weavers between each spoke. This twist moves the front weaver to the back and the back weaver to the front. Be sure that you always make the twist in the same direction, so that the pattern remains consistent. (See drawing on page 129.) Twining helps you gain control of the framework, as it holds the weaving firmly together, and bulk is added through the use of two weavers. The change from simple weaving to twining also adds variety and texture to the basket.

8. Add more ribs whenever the spaces between them become larger than 1 inch. Add ribs in pairs, so that the weaving pattern is uninterrupted. The wider your basket, the more ribs you will need. Always use fairly straight vines for ribs. As in Step 4, cut one end of the new rib on a diagonal, turn the basket upside down, and insert the cut end next to one of the spokes. Cut the other end of the rib on the diagonal, and insert it in the corresponding hole on the other side. Add a second rib in the same manner. Note that each subsequent pair of ribs will be shorter than the preceding ribs. Do not let any rib stick up past the original ribs. A nice curve

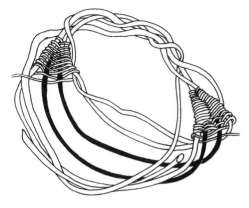

STEP 5

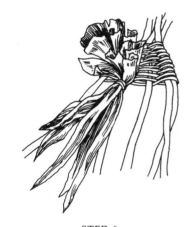

STEP 6

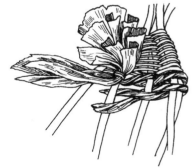

STEP 7

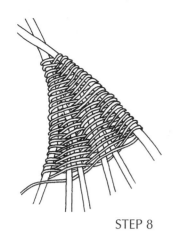

STEP 8

should form as you weave continuously from both sides toward the center bottom of the basket. It is easiest if you weave each pair of new ribs in before adding more. If only one rib is needed due to the irregularity of the vine, it's okay to add just one. If you twine at least one row, the change in weaving pattern will be unimportant.

9. The basket is finished when all the spaces are filled in. Because each vine is different, each basket is unique — a piece to be proud of!

TIPS FOR MORE BEAUTIFUL BASKETS

❦ I find it fun to weave with a variety of materials, alternating them frequently. This adds interest, color, and texture. I use anything that is flexible enough to wrap around my finger — vines of all sorts, strong leaves, small shoots or branches, barks, and so on. In one of my first all-natural baskets, I even used twisted, dead tomato plant stalks. They worked!

❦ Don't forget to add more ribs as the basket gets wider. Fewer ribs will be needed if you use thicker weavers near the bottom.

❦ Irregular spaces will develop as you progress because you are weaving a three-dimensional object and not a flat piece of cloth. The shape varies with the shape of the basket; in egg baskets, butterfly shapes appear. The use of irregular vines also causes the formation of odd, usually wedge-shaped, spaces. Fill these in with regular weaving that does not always go all the way across the basket. Weave to the point of the triangle; turn around and weave

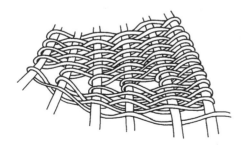

Filling irregular spaces

back. On the next row, weave to one less rib; turn around and go back. Repeat this pattern until you have no more ribs to weave over, then reverse the process, weaving to one more rib each time until you reach the point again. Repeat this process until the space is filled. As you gain confidence in this technique, you can play around with the spaces and create shapes of your own design.

❧ With irregular vine shapes, you sometimes have to add short ribs along the rim so that there is something to weave over. A single rib will alter the weaving pattern. Don't let this throw you — it is not important. Change the weaving material or twine a row to blend it in. The exciting thing about weaving with naturals is that details of the weaving are not obvious — the overall effect is what counts.

RIB-STYLE VARIATIONS

Vines can be used to make any shape basket your imagination can come up with. Do *not* fight the vine — let it help you determine the shape of your basket. In this way, your art will reflect a respect for nature. Start your framework by choosing your favorite part of the vine and considering how to showcase it. A wonderful twist could become the handle or perhaps a part of the frame that will not be woven over, but accented by the weaving.

❧ Form a melon or egg basket by placing two separate hoops at right angles.

❧ Form a flat-backed wall basket by joining a circular hoop to a D-shaped frame.

❧ Form bowl shapes or potato baskets with a single hoop to which a central rib is added by twisting a vine over on itself.

Let your imagination run wild. Try a wall hanging or sculptural piece. The same techniques work, and the vines will help with the design, if you'll let them. Have fun!

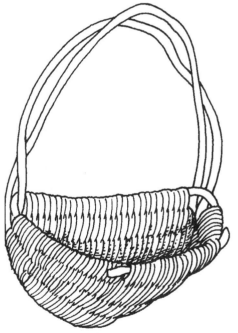

Flat-backed wall basket

HORSEHAIR BASKETRY
GERRIE KENNEDY

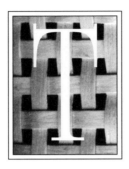he weaving projects presented in this chapter are either reproductions of, or inspired by, antique baskets. The first two are Shaker inspired and the last is a copy of a Papago Indian basket.

SHAKER BASKETRY

The Shakers were a religious communal sect held in high esteem for their philosophy of life and religion, as well as for their crafts. The Shakers strove for perfection in all aspects of their life and thus have become known for the uncompromising quality of their workmanship, design, and products, including their basketry.

Research suggests that the Shakers learned the craft of basketry from the Algonquin Indians, who were introduced to plaited splint basketry by the early European settlers. Black ash (which is used in the first two baskets in this chapter) seems to have been the preferred material of both the Native Americans and the Shakers. The Shakers, however, refined native techniques, and developed and used more sophisticated tools and machinery in their basket making. For example, the Algonquins prepared the black ash splint by pounding apart the growth rings from a log by hand, using a wooden mallet. The Shakers eventually mechanized this slow process by adapting a triphammer ordinarily used in the blacksmith shop to hammer out heated iron into shape. The consequence of the Shakers' technological improvements was to elevate their basketry to an art form that was distinctively Shaker.

A study of Shaker baskets shows the development of two major styles. First came the durable work or shop baskets, usually woven by the men. Then, when the women eventually became involved in basketry, they were responsible for developing an industry that produced more refined, often delicate household, or "fancy," baskets that were sold to the outside world.

The preparation of the black ash was painstaking, but crucial to the quality of the baskets. The yearly growth rings first were alternately pounded and peeled off the log, then cleaned to remove the somewhat "hairy" outer surface. Cleaning was achieved by sanding, scraping, or planing with a mechanical planer. Next, these growth rings were spoked and then split into halves along the grain by pulling apart each half to reveal the smooth, satiny finish of the inside wood. Last, these strips were pulled through banks of knives that cut uniform strips ready to be woven into baskets.

SOUTHWEST INDIAN BASKETRY

The last project in this chapter is a reproduction of a Papago-designed horsehair basket. This style was, and is still, typical of many Southwest tribes. It is an example of a later style of decorative basketry woven after the Native Americans had had contact with white settlers. Prior to contact with white settlers, Indian baskets were larger, made for both work and ceremonial purposes. They followed traditional shapes and designs that had been passed down from generation to generation, with little outside influence.

By the late 1800s, things began to change. A new enthusiasm for Native American baskets swept the West and Southwest. Basket collecting became a popular hobby of white tourists and settlers. In response to the influence of white aesthetics and design, basket makers in most tribes began to weave new kinds of baskets, changing and adapting forms and designs that had been used for hundreds of years. Brighter colors, marketable designs, and smaller baskets, which required less weaving time and were easier to transport, were now being woven.

It was out of this context that the Indians began to experiment with horsehair. They designed small, attractive, inexpensive baskets that are still being bought by tourists today.

SUPPLIES AND MATERIALS

The supplies you will need to make the baskets in this chapter include the following:

Scissors
Pencil
Ruler
Wood scraper (1–1½")
Bread board (or small piece of wood)
Mold for Shaker basket
Soup bowl
Tacks
Sewing needle for elastic thread
Extra-fine sandpaper
Blow dryer

Of these, the most important basket-making aid for the Shaker projects is the wooden mold. Most Shaker molds were made of pine or maple. Although they were usually turned on a lathe, they can also be made by cutting out blanks the shape of the basket you wish to make. The bottom angle is then created by first sanding with a power sander and then filing and sanding by hand until the finished form is obtained. Some of my most cherished and well-made molds were created exactly this way by an artist friend, who used a minimum of woodworking tools. (The baskets presented here are designed to fit the dimensions of the molds that I supply (for address, see page 151). If you make your own mold or buy a mold from another supplier, you may have to increase or decrease the number of uprights or spokes given in the project directions. When you make this adjustment, be sure to place the uprights fairly close together. If you use too few uprights, your basket will not have enough support and will be flimsy.)

PREPARING THE HORSEHAIR

The horsehair used in all three of these baskets needs to be long and of good quality, although each project requires a relatively small amount of hair. The hair must be from the horse's tail; mane hair is not long enough. It can be cut from the tail or collected from a brush after brushing the tail. You can also purchase horsehair (see page 151).

Both collected and purchased hair should be washed with any mild shampoo and rinsed in warm water. Cut off badly discolored (manure-stained) ends. Hang to dry.

PREPARING BLACK ASH SPLINTS

Authentic Shaker baskets must be constructed of splint from a black ash tree (*Fraxinus nigra*). Splint can be obtained from local or mail-order basketry suppliers (see page 151) or, if you wish to start from scratch, from a tree that you fell. If you purchase splint (by far the simpler way), be certain that you are getting *pounded* splint, rather than planed or sawn material, which is dry, brittle, and difficult to work with. Planed and pounded splint can be quickly differentiated by observing the splint's texture: Planed splint has a smooth finish, and pounded growth rings are rough and hairy in appearance.

Black ash trees are found in northeastern North America from Newfoundland to Manitoba, south to Delaware, and west to Iowa. Look for them in wet soils bordering swamps or in lowlands where drainage is poor. Black ash resembles the larger and more common white ash, although the top branches of black ash are heavier looking. In addition, the crown of black ash typically consists of only four or five thick branches with a limited number of short, fat secondary twigs, giving it a scraggly appearance compared to white ash. The gray to gray-green bark of black ash is not as furrowed as that of white ash, and bits of it will flake or fall off when you rub it with your hand. Choose a 9- to 12-inch diameter tree that is straight and knot-free; after felling it, cut the trunk into a log at least 6 feet long.

Before the growth rings can be pounded apart, you must first remove the bark from the log with a drawknife. After the log is free of bark, pound it with a wooden mallet or maul, beginning at one end and slowly moving to the other with overlapping blows — about fifteen to twenty per inch. When one year's layer begins to separate, pull it off and let it air dry for twenty-four hours before coiling it up and storing it for later use. It takes several days to separate all of the growth rings in this manner. Keep the tree moist between pounding sessions by covering it with canvas and leaving it in the shade, or by submerging it in water.

Removing bark with a draw knife

Pounding the log

Separating of one-year growth layer

Both purchased and hand-pounded splints must be divided in half lengthwise to expose the inner "satin" wood. Begin by soaking the splints in cool water for twenty-four hours. Score a splint with a utility knife, going halfway through the thickness of the wood. Next, gently bend the scored wood until the growth ring divides in half, allowing you to get a firm grasp on both pieces. Applying even pressure on both halves of the splint, use your thumbs and fists to pull the two halves evenly apart with a rolling motion. Keep both halves as even as possible. If one side of the splint becomes thinner, pull more firmly on the opposite side to even out the thickness.

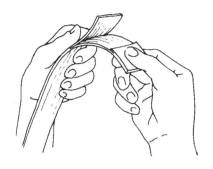

Bending the scored wood

Next, you must clean the rough side of the newly divided splints. This is traditionally accomplished by placing a piece of leather over your thigh, holding one end of the splint firmly over your leg, and scraping it with a jackknife. A more efficient technique is to flatten the splint against a work surface and go over it with a 1- or 1½-inch wood scraper. You may clean it further with a piece of fine-grade sandpaper, if you wish.

Scissors are usually used to cut the splints into the desired widths (see project instructions below), but I have found that such unlikely "woodworking tools" as leather-cutting tools or a pasta cutter make multiple strips smoothly, evenly, and quickly. Don't be afraid to experiment with untraditional tools. Whatever you use, be sure to cut your widths as evenly as possible.

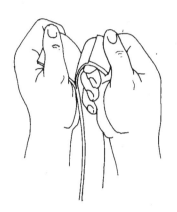

Pulling the halves apart

Before attempting to prepare your splint from scratch, be advised: it is back-breaking work. Given the small amounts of ash in these projects, it would be far easier to purchase prepared ¹⁄₁₆, ³⁄₃₂-, and ⅛-inch satin splint from a supplier.

SHAKER BASKETS: BEFORE YOU BEGIN

An important part of Shaker basketry is the cleaning of the material. The small baskets described here need ash that is about the thickness of two pieces of construction paper.

Before beginning any project, identify the smooth (satiny) side of the splints. (The satin finish should always appear on the outside of the basket.) Lay the splint on a wooden board, rough side up, and scrape it with a wood scraper, using long, even strokes. Give it a final smoothing by rubbing it with sandpaper.

Before you begin to weave, use a wood scraper or jackknife to scrape one-third of the thickness off the last inch (or a length that will span about four uprights) on both ends of all weavers. By tapering the ends in this way, you can eliminate any bumps or bulges where the ends overlap when you must add new weavers.

When you are ready to weave, quickly dip into tepid water the materials you will be working with. Do not soak materials in water. Whenever you begin a new weaver, it, too, should be quickly dipped into water.

To add a new ash weaver, cut the old weaver so that it ends *on top* of an upright, and weave it in to its end. Count back four uprights from where the old weaver ends and begin the new weaver in the following manner: With the satin side facing out, tuck the end of the new weaver under an upright on top of the old weaver, and continue weaving over the old weaver.

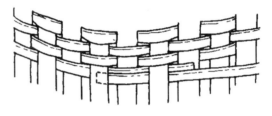

Adding a weaver

When you add horsehair weavers, it is most important to keep the tension taut. Cut the end of the previous horsehair weaver so it ends *underneath* an upright; leave a 1-inch tail on the outside of the basket. Begin the new weaver three uprights back from this tail, weave one complete row, and then slowly pull on the weaver until the short end disappears under the first spoke. Weave another row before gently increasing tension on the weaver. Achieving the proper tension will require some practice. Although you must maintain an even tension, if you get the weaver too taut, the weaver may pull right off the mold.

SPOON BASKET
2" wide x 3" long x 1¼" high

*The Shakers called this type basket a "fancy basket." Its name is
probably derived from its oval shape, which somewhat resembles a
spoon. Some of these baskets were filled with stuffing so that they
could be used as pincushions; others were fastened to the inside of
longer baskets or oval boxes to hold sewing notions.
This basket is shown on color page 94.*

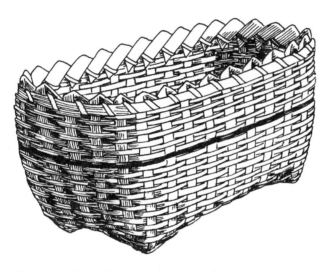

This basket is shown on color page 94.

1. Obtain purchased splint or prepare the splint as described on pages 138–39. As you weave, be sure that the satin finish is always on the outside of the basket.

2. Scrape or sand the rough side of the fourteen uprights (both 5¼ and 7¼ inch) until they are about the thickness of two pieces of construction paper.

3. Dip all materials quickly in tepid water so that they are less brittle.

4. With the satin sides facing up, lay three of the 7¼-inch uprights horizontally on a flat surface. They should be parallel to each other, approximately ¹⁄₁₆ inch apart. Center a 5¼-inch upright across these vertically, and weave it through in a one over, one under pattern.

5. Weave in the remaining 5¼-inch uprights on each side of this center to create a mat with three 7¼-inch horizontal uprights and

MATERIALS

Black ash:
   Five ⅛" wide splints, 7¼"
   long (uprights)

   Nine ⅛" wide splints, 5¼"
   long (uprights)

   Approximately 60 feet, ¹⁄₃₂"
   wide (weavers)

   One ¹⁄₁₆" wide splint, 9"
   long (rim)

   One ¹⁄₁₆" wide splint, 20"
   long (lashing)

Black horsehair:
   Approximately 10 long
   strands (weavers)

Mold: 3" x 1⅞" (top
diameter) x 1½" high

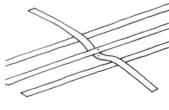

STEP 4

nine 5¼-inch vertical uprights. Measure the bottom length of the mold, and adjust the spokes of your mat so that they will fit over it.

6. To complete the bottom, weave in the two remaining 7¼-inch spokes horizontally. Measure the bottom width of the mold, and adjust the spokes so that the mat will fit the bottom of the mold exactly.

7. Place this woven bottom over the base of the mold, satin side up. Secure firmly against mold by placing tacks in each of the four corners and in the center of the mold. Place the tacks between the spokes to avoid damaging the splint. With a rubber band, secure the uprights against the mold. Space the uprights evenly, and push the two corner uprights toward each other. Allow to dry in a warm or sunny spot, so that when the rubber band is removed, the uprights will conform to the shape of the mold.

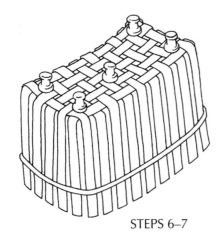

STEPS 6–7

8. Remove the rubber band from the mold. Choose a long ¹⁄₃₂-inch splint weaver, find its center, and using scissors, taper it for 1 inch, just off center. Dip it quickly in tepid water to dampen it.

9. Fold the tapered weaver in half and loop it around a corner spoke, satin side out. Take one of the ends and begin weaving over and under the uprights along one side of the mold. Be certain that the satin side of the weaver is facing out.

10. Take the other half of the weaver and give it a full twist, so that its satin side is facing out. Weave with this upright in the same direction as you wove in Step 9, weaving over the spokes you wove under in that step. This row will lock in all uprights on the side.

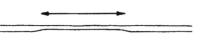

STEP 8

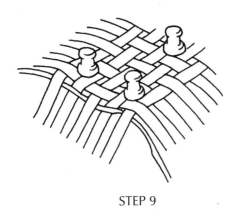

STEP 9

STEP 10

Continue in this manner all the way around the bottom, weaving first one weaver and then the other, until two full rows

are completed. This technique is called chase weave because one weaver is always "chasing" the other, but never passing it.

11. Chase weave around the mold, applying slight pressure against the uprights to conform to the sides of the mold, until the basket is approximately ⅞ inch high. Pack down each row as you weave.

Note: While weaving the first eight or ten rows, be sure to pinch or gather the corners together to encourage equal spacing between the spokes. Use water sparingly on *weavers*, but to avoid breaking the *spokes*, keep them just damp by moistening them lightly with dampened fingers.

12. Before you can weave in the horsehair, you must first cut and taper the ends of the ash weavers for ½ inch, so that they end staggered three or four uprights apart, above where you initially started the weaving.

13. Dry the partially completed basket on the mold for several hours in a sunny, warm place, or dry it with a blow dryer set on warm for three or four minutes. Drying the weavers will shrink them. Again, pack down the rows of weavers, and compact them against the bottom of the mold.

14. To begin weaving with horsehair, secure the first and second pieces of hair just above the tapered ends of ash weavers as described on page 140.

15. Chase weave a horsehair band ⅛ to ¼ inch high. Remember to keep a firm tension. End the horsehairs about three uprights apart, with each end under an upright.

16. Weave the remainder of the basket with black ash. Start with two pieces, each having its end tapered for ½ inch. Count back three uprights from the end of each horsehair and add the new weavers. Chase weave in the ash to the desired height of the basket (the band will be approximately ⅜ inch wide).

17. Stagger the ends three or four uprights apart, taper, and level the basket by eye.

18. Remove the basket from the mold, and place it in a small box with a hole cut in the top. Position a blow dryer next to the box, with its tip pointed into the hole. Dry on low for fifteen minutes. Pack weavers gently.

RIM AND LASHING

19. Thoroughly clean and sand the 1/16-inch rim and 1/16-inch lashing. Dip both in water to saturate.

20. Carefully dip the spokes of the basket in tepid water. *Do not get any of the weavers wet.* Wipe any excess water from spokes *before* turning right side up, to avoid swelling of weavers.

21. Cut uprights 1/2 inch high above the last row of weaving. Insert lashing down the back of a spoke and under three or four rows of weavers, satin side facing out.

22. Place the rim directly above and resting on top of the last row of weavers *on the outside of the basket.*

23. Bring the lashing up over the top of the rim and around to the front. Go under the rim and between the uprights, pulling it snugly to the inside toward the bottom of basket. Next, *go back* and take the upright to the left of lashing, and bend it against the basket body with the lashing as you take the lashing over the rim and around the next space between the uprights. Continue around three sides of basket.

24. When you get near the point where you began, cut the rim so that the ends overlap for a span of four uprights. Continue to bend down the uprights and fasten them inside with the lashing. Since the rim ends overlap, you must now go under the rim and through the basket to sew it closed.

25. End the piece of lashing as you began. Secure the last bent-down upright, and carry the lashing down behind an upright and under four rows of weavers.

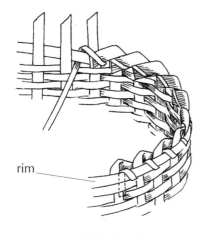

rim

STEP 22–23

SHAKER HORSEHAIR BASKET

1⅝" diameter x 1½" high

This basket (shown on color page 94) is inspired by one in the collection of the United Society of Shakers, Sabbathday Lake, Maine. An example of the later type of Shaker basketry known as "fancy basketry," the original is delicate and striking for its beauty; it shows the hand of a skilled weaver.

The idea of weaving a kittenhead out of horsehair is adapted here to fit on a reproduction of a Hancock (Massachusetts) Shaker Village mold. The original basket is modified here in an attempt to simplify a somewhat slow and tedious basket to make.

MATERIALS

Black ash:
   fourteen ¹⁄₁₆" wide splints, 4I" long (uprights)

   one ³⁄₃₂" wide splint, 7½" long (rim)

   one ¹⁄₁₆" wide splint, 16" long (lashing)

White horsehair: small bunch (50-60 strands) (weavers)

Black horsehair: small bunch (50-60 strands) (weavers)

Mold: 3" wide (top diameter) x 2" high

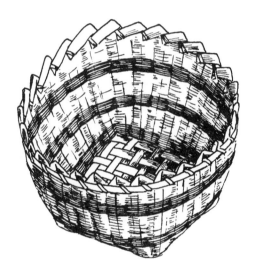

1. Prepare the splint as described on pages 138–39. As you weave, be sure that the satin finish is always on the outside of the basket.

2. Scrape or sand the rough side of the fourteen uprights until they are about the thickness of two pieces of construction paper, as described on page 139.

3. Dip all materials quickly in tepid water, so that they are less brittle.

4. With the satin sides facing up, lay three uprights vertical and parallel on a flat surface. Weave a fourth upright across these three, dividing them exactly in half.

STEP 6

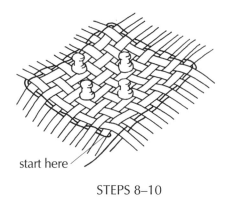

start here

STEPS 8–10

5. Weave in three uprights on each side of this horizontal. Adjust the spokes as necessary, so that what you have woven will fit perfectly within the width of the square on the bottom of your mold.

6. Weave in the four remaining uprights vertically, and adjust these, too, to fit the mold. You now have a woven square consisting of fourteen uprights. Be sure the uprights are spaced evenly within the square.

7. Dampen the uprights around the outer perimeter of the square. Turn the square over, so that the rough side faces up. Place a ruler over the woven portion, with the edge of the ruler lined up against the edge of the weaving. Bending against the ruler, make 90-degree-angle folds in the *two* uprights adjacent to each corner. Follow this procedure on the other three sides, so that sixteen corner uprights are bent up. Leave the middle three uprights on each side unbent.

8. Lay the woven bottom over the base of the mold, satin side facing out. Secure the woven piece firmly against the mold with three or four tacks positioned toward the center of the mold; leave the corners free, so that you can later push them up to form the base — the "cat ears" — of the basket. Place the tacks *between* the uprights, to avoid damaging the splints. With a rubber band, secure the uprights against the mold. (See Steps 6–7, page 142.) Space the uprights evenly, and push the two corner uprights toward each other. Allow to dry in a warm or sunny spot, so that when the rubber band is removed, the uprights will conform to the shape of the mold. Remove the rubber band from the mold.

9. Prepare the horsehair as described on pages 137–38.

10. Begin to weave in horsehair, remembering that the predominant background color should be white with three bands of black. Choose a long black hair, and fold it in half, about 2 inches off center (so each strand ends at a different point on the mold). Loop it around a corner spoke. Take one of the ends and begin weaving over and under the uprights once around the mold. Use firm tension. Pick up the other weaver, and weave with it, chase fashion.

Note: It is most important to keep tension on the active weaver. At the same time, attempt to keep tension on the other weaver as well.

FIRST BAND OF BLACK

11. Weave the next thirteen rows (about ⅛ inch), gathering and pushing the four corner uprights closer together as you weave. This will adjust and even the spacing between the uprights and create the "cat ears" on the bottom of your basket. Keep both weavers taut, and press the uprights against the body of the mold as you weave. Add weavers whenever necessary as described on page 140.

STEP 11

FIRST BAND OF WHITE

12. By now, spacing should be even between the uprights. Occasional adjustments will be necessary, however, to keep even spacing and to keep the corner uprights slightly fanning out from the center on each of the four sides of the basket. Add your first white horsehair, weaving a complete row, and then add a second white horsehair as described on page 140. Weave until the white band is ³⁄₁₆ inch wide.

REMAINING BANDS OF COLOR

13. Add black horsehairs, as in Step 12. Weave until band is ⅛ inch wide, and then weave five or six additional rows of horsehair.

14. Add white horsehair as before, and weave a band ³⁄₁₆ inch wide. Weave five or six additional rows of horsehair.

15. Add black horsehairs, and weave a band ³⁄₁₆ inch wide.

16. Add white horsehairs, and weave a band ⅛ inch wide.

RIM AND LASHING

17. Follow Steps 19–25, page 144, *except* use the ³⁄₃₂-inch rim and the ¹¹⁄₁₆-inch wide lashing.

COILED HORSEHAIR BASKET
1½" diameter x 1" high

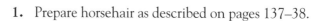

GERRIE KENNEDY

MATERIALS

Bunch of horsehair about the thickness of your pinky finger

This is a reproduction of a basket made by the Papago Indians of the Southwest. Small baskets like this were made in response to a great influx of settlers and tourists into the area in the late 1800s. Native Americans throughout the West realized they could participate in and draw income from this tourist economy. In response, they began to weave new types of basketry using nontraditional materials and forms. The following (shown also on color page 94) is an example of such a basket.

Throughout the coiling of this basket, keep firm tension on the horsehair you are stitching with. It is most difficult to keep proper tension during the start of the basket, but it does become easier by the second or third round.

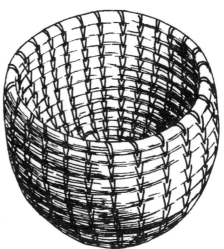

1. Prepare horsehair as described on pages 137–38.

2. Thread a sewing needle with two long horsehairs to make a double strand.

3. Hold a bunch of horsehair (about thirty hairs) in your left hand. Point the short end to the right. Lay the tail ends of the threaded hair along the bundle to be coiled, and wrap it in such a way that you make a knot ½ inch from the short end.

4. Begin wrapping and bending the bundle as shown for about two-thirds of an inch. Wrap the hairs with firm pressure and place

STEP 3

wrapping hairs close together.

5. Bend and fold this wrapped section to form the center round of your basket. Incorporate the ½-inch tail from the beginning into the main coil as you create the circle.

6. Push the needle from the back to the front up through the center hole. Wrap two or three more times, around the bundle, and then take the needle through the center again. Repeat wrapping and coming through the center, until you have gone once around (counterclockwise).

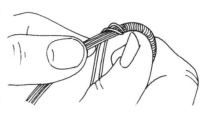

STEP 4

7. From this point, you will *discontinue to wrap* the bundle, and just sew. You are now ready to add approximately twenty hairs to the inside wall of the bundle, next to stitches, so that when the bundle is sewn together it creates a coil 3/32 inch wide. Add hairs, about ten at a time, throughout the coiling process. Keep the thickness of the coil uniform, and hide the ends of newly added hairs.

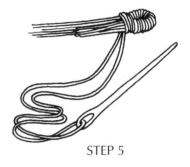

STEP 5

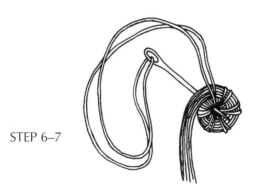

STEP 6–7

8. Begin to sew a second round, but change your stitches so that the needle now goes through the *upper half of the coil below* it, rather than through the center hole. Keep the sewing hairs taut, and place stitches about 1/16 inch apart. Complete the second round.

9. The third round—and all remaining rounds—is made with a **split stitch,** which is done by sewing between the stitches of the previous round. Your basket will look neater if, rather than piercing through the middle of the coil and thread, you pierce through the *top of the coil,* catching only eight or nine hairs.

As you progress, the diameter of the base increases, which also increases the space between the stitches. You will therefore need to increase the number of stitches in each round in order to retain the 1/16-inch spacing between stitches. Do this by taking an extra stitch through the top third of the coil below, between the split stitches. On the next round, you will split through these additional stitches as with the others.

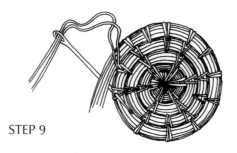

STEP 9

10. When the diameter of the base is 1 inch, begin to build up the sides of the basket. To form the desired bowl shape, overlap each succeeding row of coil a little farther toward the inside, so it sits slightly *on top* of the previous row.

11. Continue to increase the overlap for several rows until one coil sits directly above the next. Work until basket is 1 inch high.

12. To finish the edge of the basket, taper off the horsehairs at a gradual angle covering a span of ½ inch. Continue to stitch the coil in smaller and finer stitches until the end is covered and sewn down.

13. Fasten off the stitching strand by carrying it down through the inside of the coil for about ½ inch, and hiding it inside the middle of the bottom coil. Snip end.

BASKETRY SUPPLIERS

Basket Beginnings
25 West Tioga Street
Tunkhannock, PA 18657
717-836-6080
800-82-FIBER
*Pine needles, raffia, dracena
and other hand-gathered
materials*

Basketworks
2671 State Road, 25 N.
Lafayette, IN 47905
317-742-5121

Connecticut Cane and Reed
Box 762
Manchester, CT 06040
203-646-6586

Gerrie Kennedy
Berkshire Basketry
P.O. Box 85
Worthington, MA 01098
413-238-5816
*Black ash splints, kits, molds,
horsehair*

H.H. Perkins Co.
10 South Bradley Road
Woodbridge, CT 06525
203-389-9501
800-462-6660

Jeannie McFarland
Baskets and Bullets
P.O. Box 19149
Thorne Bay, AK 99919
907-828-3355
Teneriffes

John E. McGuire Basket
  Supplies
398 South Main Street
Geneva, NY 14456
315-781-1251
*Black ash splint, basket molds,
tools*

North Carolina Basket Works
P.O. Box 1438
Sanford, NC 27331
919-775-7976
800-338-4972

GLOSSARY

Basket weight. Any heavy object, such as a book or rock, used to put pressure on an area of a basket in order to hold the shape.

Bee skep. A dome-shaped basket, formerly used as a bee hive.

Butt ends. The thicker bottom or base sections of such materials as willow, twigs, or branches. Can also refer to the joining of two end pieces by letting them meet without overlapping.

Buttonhole stitch. A stitch done in coiled baskets to form a reinforced edge; can cover the coil material completely or leave some exposed.

Bye stakes. Spokes inserted next to existing spokes to form a working pair. Also, an extra spoke placed in the basket framework to make an odd number of spokes and enable a continuous weave.

Chase weave. A method of weaving in which two weavers or sets of weavers are woven alternately around a basket; the second weaver never overtakes the first.

Double spoke. Two side-by-side spokes used as a pair.

Feeding the tail. In coil basketry, the process of sliding a bundle of core material through a ring-type gauge in order to maintain an even thickness.

Fern stitch. A variation of the wheat stitch in which a diagonal stitch is placed to the side of each wheat stitch; when completed, the stitching is fernlike. *See also* Wheat stitch.

Foot border. A practical and decorative border added to the bottom of a finished basket or woven as part of the basket base. The foot border carries the weight of the basket, sparing wear and tear and easily repaired or replaced.

French rand. A type of weave in which each row begins at an angle to the one below it, thus forming a spiral or diagonal design. Traditionally used in willow work to make use of shorter rods.

Gauge. A guide that maintains a consistent thickness of the coiling material.

Lashing. Material used to wrap and secure the rim pieces of a basket together.

Prick up. Puncture spokes with a knife point in order to encourage them to bend without splitting.

Randing. A simple over-and-under weave done with a single weaver.

Rapping iron. A small hammer, short length of narrow pipe, or other slender tool heavy enough to beat down the weaving.

Slype. Create a point on the end of a spoke by trimming it at an angle with scissors or a knife.

Splice. The point at which two pieces join with overlapping ends; the ends can be slanted or slyped to make the overlap less bulky and obvious.

Spokes. Pieces that form the framework of the basket and upon which weavers are woven over and under. Spokes usually radiate outward from a circle. Also referred to as *ribs* or *stakes*.

Spoke weight. A gauge that measures the distance each spoke must be bent.

Start. The completely wrapped, beginning section of core material, around which the coil is built.

Start-and-stop weaving. A kind of weaving in which a new weaver is used for each successive row of weaving around a basket.

Stook. An upright bundle of hay, tied at the middle; a haystack.

Stool. On shrubs, the stump from which multiple new growth appears in spring.

Teneriffe. A decorative embroidery technique in which a lacelike pattern is woven within a ring or other space.

Trac border. A decorative weaving pattern that forms the rim of a basket; the weave uses an over two, under two, over one, under one, over one, and under one progression that angles down toward the weaving.

Triple weave. A weaving pattern that uses three weavers simultaneously. Working from left to right, each weaver goes over the other two weavers in the triplet, in front of two spokes, behind one spoke, and out to the front again.

Twine. A weave done with two weavers simultaneously; the two cross each other as they weave around each spoke. Particularly good for strengthening and shaping.

Upright. Spokes that form the basket sides.

Upset. Bend base spokes upward to form side uprights.

Wale. Weave.

Weaver. The material that is used for the weaving.

Wheat stitch. A decorative stitch used to hold the rows of core material together in coiled baskets. One part of the stitch is vertical; the other is at a diagonal. Resembles a small shaft of wheat.

Willow brake. A tool consisting of two metal prongs arranged in a V shape and used to strip bark from willow rods.

Withe. A long slender twig or branch; usually refers to willow branches.

INDEX

Page numbers in *italics* refer to photographs or tables.